10.98

DATE DUE			

THE ART OF
LANDSCAPE
AND
SEASCAPE
PAINTING

THE ART OF
LANDSCAPE
AND
SEASCAPE
PAINTING

Gerald Woods

Crescent Books
New York

Design Manager: Hans Verkroost
Design: Ross George
Editor: Sandy Shepherd
Production: Peter Phillips
            Stewart Bowling

The 1989 edition is published by Crescent Books,
distributed by Crown Publishers, Inc.,
225 Park Avenue South, New York, New York 10003

Edited and designed by the Artists House Division
of Mitchell Beazley International Ltd
Artists House, 14-15 Manette Street, London W1V 5LB

ISBN 0-517-66300-7

Typeset by Hourds Typographica, Stafford
Origination by La Cromolito s.n.c., Milan
Printed in Portugal by Printer Portuguesa Lda.

h g f e d c b a

CONTENTS

INTRODUCTION 6

HISTORY AND BACKGROUND 8

MATERIALS AND TECHNIQUES 14
  Paper 16
  Drawing Techniques 18
  Charcoal 20
  Pastels 22
  Pen and Ink 24
  Drawing for Painting 28
  Sketchbooks 30
  Brushes 32
  Watercolour 34
  Gouache 40
  Supports 42
  Oil and Acrylic 44
  Easels 46
  Colour 48

APPROACHING THE SUBJECT 50
  Composition 52
  Light, Mood and Atmosphere 58
  Working on Location 64
  White Cliffs 66
  Swiss Lakes 72
  Venice 78
  Athens 80
  Egypt 82
  Tuscany 84
  Landscape and Industry 86
  Buildings in Landscape 90
  Clouds, Sky and the Sea 94
  Trees 98
  Rivers 100
  Beach Scenes 102

MOUNTING AND FRAMING 106

  Glossary 108
  Index 110

INTRODUCTION

The things that we desire most are not outside us, they are inside us – the idea of the beauty of a landscape, for example, comes from within us. When we project ourselves into a landscape, we find that it reflects something of our own being. The drawing or painting of a landscape becomes a visible means of expressing our emotional response to that particular place. Nostalgia for one's homeland is one of the deepest of human sentiments. The places one knows best can, as William Winter said, inspire a "tranquil sadness which is stronger than happiness".

The poet Paul Valéry asks of himself "What do you like then?", and answers "I like to believe that I see things no one has seen in the things that everybody sees . . ."This, in essence, is what we should be attempting to do when we produce a landscape painting – to uncover things that are unseen because they are not perceived by anyone else.

This book introduces techniques which will enable you to say something about a landscape or seascape. The key to all serious landscape painting is communication – if a painting does not communicate, it is useless, no matter how much technical virtuosity it demonstrates.

But I hope that you will not be detained too long by this book, or any other. Much better, as Cézanne said, to "read" nature, to "let us realize our sensations in an aesthetic that is at once personal and traditional. The strongest will be he who sees most deeply . . ."

HISTORY AND BACKGROUND

Landscape painting has its origins in Egyptian wall and papyrus paintings and in Roman frescoes. As a prime subject for painting, however, its earliest appearance is in China, during the Tang dynasty (618–907AD). A glimpse through the history of the subject will show you that there are many ways of treating a landscape.

In medieval Europe, landscape was restricted to the leafy ornamental designs that decorated manuscripts. It also appeared in agricultural scenes in calendars and Books of Hours, such as the one illustrated by the Limbourg brothers for the Duke of Berry (begun in 1413). But landscape then was essentially symbolic and subordinate to the religious theme — even in paintings. Not surprisingly, many artists were reluctant to confine their observations of nature to mere decoration; in the paintings of Simone Martini (c.1284–1344), for example, there is no doubt that, although his task lay in conveying the Christian message, there is a sensuous delight in nature, many direct references to which appear in the background.

The first true landscapes in Europe were painted for the manuscript known as the *Hours of Turin* (c.1420), thought to be by Jan van Eyck. They are quite small in scale — roughly 8×5cm ($3\frac{1}{2} \times 2$in). But perhaps the works that

Rembrandt's *The Stone Bridge*, **below left**, and Thomas Girtin's *Kirkstall Abbey*, **right**, show how far landscape painting had come in 300 years, when compared with the illustration from the *Luttrell Psalter*, **below right**, c.1340. Rembrandt's interest is in the way the light dominates the scene, guiding the spectator's eye into the landscape from left to right, across the bridge, and into the centre of the painting. Girtin's watercolour uses monochromatic colour and broad washes to unify the scene and convey a sense of harmony. The heavily textured paper softens the forms and enhances the tranquillity of the scene.

best represent the growing curiosity surrounding landscape at this time were the topographical watercolours of Innsbruck painted by Albrecht Dürer (1471–1528), on his travels across the Alps into Italy. Their attention to botanical detail made them almost like still-lifes.

The introduction of perspective in painting in the fifteenth century, a taste for the classical rules of harmony and proportion, and the popularity of classical subject matter, led to an order in the perception and rendering of landscape subjects, which lasted until the eighteenth century. Artists such as Giorgione, Claude and Poussin were experts at harnessing the elements of nature to fit their classical compositions. Giorgione (c.1476–1510), in common with other Venetian painters of the period, was inspired by the idyllic stories of the Greek poets. However, he was more interested in conveying the mood of a landscape than in narrative. He was also one of the first Venetians to paint oils on a small scale for the private collector rather than for churches.

Claude Lorraine (1600–82) painted romantic views of the Roman Campagna, the plains and hills around Rome. He approached most of his landscapes in the same way, organizing them like a stage set: a dark green foreground with a large clump of trees on one side and a smaller clump on the other; a lighter green middle ground containing some element such as a bridge or a farm building; and a bluish background with rivers or mountains. The figures were then arranged and rearranged within this composition.

The paintings of Nicolas Poussin

(1594–1665) are characterized by a flattened perspective which creates a sculptural, frieze-like quality in which all the forms are closely related. Poussin believed that the colour and pattern in a painting should be subordinate to the narrative expressed by the figures; by understating them he emphasized the two-dimensionality of the painting.

There were notable exceptions to the formality of the classical approach, such as the Dutch painter Pieter Brueghel (c.1525–1569), whose landscapes were far less stylized and more spontaneous than those of his Italian and French contemporaries – a result of his astute, honest observations of nature.

The practice of painting from direct observation, in the open air, really only started in the seventeenth century, with Dutch painters. Then, artists did not have the convenience of paint contained in tubes which could be squeezed onto the palette at will. Instead, drawings were made directly in crayon or pen and were later painted up in oil in the studio. Even so, Rembrandt (1606–1669) produced on site some of the most spontaneous landscape

views, in his small etchings of Dutch rivers and canals. Other Dutch painters, however, such as Ruysdael, Seghers and Hobbema, accepted commissions to produce idealized views of known places, which were usually completed in the studio. Salomon van Ruysdael (c.1600–70) painted landscapes near his native Haarlem. The subtle balance of light and shade in his forest scenes revealed for the first time the poetic quality of the northern landscape. Landscape paintings by Hercules Seghers (c.1589–c.1638) show him to be a master of fantasy in that he frequently invented the scenes and their effects of light. His etchings and drawings, however, are full of carefully observed factual detail. Meindert Hobbema (1638–1709), painting thirty years later, produced gentle, romantic landscapes, often containing water mills, which had none of the fantasy of Seghers' landscapes.

Working in the open air, painters became more aware of the beauty of skies and light. This is obvious in the works of the Dutch painters of this time. Aelbert Cuyp (1620–91), for example, in his seascapes and landscapes, shows a great interest in the play of light, and

Above: Constable's sketches of the landscape he knew so well are deceptive in terms of the way the paint has been handled. The brushwork is very fluid and the paint loosely applied, even flicked onto the canvas in areas just to hint at light striking leaves and water. His interest in light and colour was to influence the Impressionists almost a century later.

Simon Vlieger (1601–53) was expert at conveying the atmosphere of sea and sky.

Almost a century later, the Venetian painter Canaletto (1697–1768), working in Venice and London, used a device called a *camera obscura* which reflects a view from a mirror through a lens to the surface of a canvas or paper. This method lent paintings a heightened sense of realism and was soon adopted by other artists.

English artists were among the first to produce landscape paintings entirely out of doors. John Robert Cozens (1752–1797) and Thomas Girtin (1775–1802) were both watercolourists whose work paralleled the sentimental poetry of Wordsworth in celebrating the awesome grandeur of spectacular scenery.

Mont Ste-Victoire was one of Cézanne's favourite themes, to which he returned time and time again. Although he was a contemporary of the Impressionists, and was greatly influenced by their ideas, he never really associated with their movement. His paintings combine the classical emphasis on structure with the Impressionists' sense of light and colour.

Turner took the landscapist's interest in the sky and light to new extremes. Here, in *Snowstorm, or Hannibal and his army crossing the Alps*, the threatening landscape is made even more so by the looming storm poised, like an enormous wave, to crash down on the figures below.

Sir William Coldstream's oil painting of the casualty reception station at Capua, in Italy, was painted in his capacity as War Artist during the Second World War. His principal interest is in the tents, as blocks of colour, set against the backdrop of the town's buildings. The only "natural" landscape element is the mountain range in the distance. In this respect it is a townscape, rather than a landscape in the classical sense.

The influence of the Impressionists is evident in Vuillard's *Landscape — House on the Left*. It has the casual view of a photograph, rather than being classically composed, with part of the house coming in from the left and the edge of a wooden balcony visible in the foreground. He has also used complementary colours, making the shadow in the foreground purple to contrast with the yellows in the image. His textured use of gouache creates patterns in what would otherwise be flat patches of colour.

Aptly named *The Quiet River*, what gives Victor Pasmore's oil painting its sense of peace is the soft and minimal use of colour and the horizontal and vertical lines that impose a simplicity on the scene. This lyrical style is characteristic of Pasmore's early landscapes, which were later to become abstract.

The nineteenth century saw a change in attitude towards the status of landscape painting, which was probably influenced by the works of John Constable (1776–1837) and William Turner (1775–1851). Constable cast aside the classical constraints on landscape compositions imposed by Claude and Poussin, and painted what he saw with his own eyes — rustic elements such as cottages, carts and haystacks. Whereas most of Constable's paintings were produced within a few square miles of his native Dedham in East Anglia, Turner produced most of his work on his many excursions through England, France, Switzerland and Italy. He produced some 19,000 drawings and watercolours, many of which (sometimes called "colour beginnings) have a timeless quality which makes them as relevant today as they were over a hundred years ago. Turner was obsessed with light and the way it diffuses colour, to the extent that the landscape itself became of secondary importance; in some scenes the landscape elements are scarcely visible through the mists or clouds of colour.

In France, twenty years later, artists such as Corot (1796–1875) were rejecting academic rules and working directly from nature, possibly influenced by Constable and Turner. But even though Corot portrayed light and form in a new way, his paintings were still underpinned by a strong sense of the classical tradition.

The revolution in painting came with the Impressionists and Post-Impressionists, who have perhaps had the greatest impact on the way that we approach landscape painting today. Monet, Pissarro, Renoir, Van Gogh and others, were all *plein-airistes* (open air painters) who tried to capture in their paintings the many moods and qualities of light and colour in a landscape as they experienced it directly. In particular, they analyzed colour and light as reflected off water and other surfaces. Their ideas were borrowed from physicists such as Chevreul, who were developing theories of light and colour. One of the most influential of these theories was that any object casts a shadow in its complementary colour. The emphasis the Impressionists gave to light meant that form in

their paintings was often not clearly defined, which was a source of much criticism.

Cézanne (1839–1906) brought definition back into landscape painting by starting with the form of objects and then using colour to model them and give them expression.

The influence of the French School is still very much evident in landscape painting today, in the way painters apply colour and analyze their subject. Some artists today have progressed from traditional interpretations to an abstract concept of natural forms. The work of Victor Pasmore (b.1910), for instance, shows the gradual evolution of an artist working from the direct tradition of Constable and Turner, towards abstract harmonies which have their source in natural forms.

Landscapes and seascapes will always be popular subjects, because in painting them the artist is in closest contact with nature than with any other subject. I suggest that you look at the works of the Masters and use them to fire your imagination and stimulate new ideas for tackling the subject.

MATERIALS
AND
TECHNIQUES

The landscape painter today is faced with a
bewildering variety of materials and equipment,
much of which is very costly. Money alone will
not turn a novice into an expert, but not even a
professional will cope with inadequate materials.
In this section you will find a range of materials
and media discussed for use in drawing or
painting your landscape. It is important,
however, to remember that paints, canvas,
brushes, paper and so on, have just one
purpose – to enable you to produce the kind of
painting you want. If exactly what you are aiming
for can be achieved with, say, gouache and
cardboard, then you would be wasting your time
and money buying an expensive handmade
paper. If, however, you need to lay a number of
washes and later scrub out and remove certain
passages of a painting, then a good-quality
watercolour paper will be invaluable.

PAPER

Choosing the right paper to work on is very much a matter of personal preference, but also depends on the medium you use. Some people like the texture of a rough paper, others prefer the smoothness of Hot-pressed paper. I happen to dislike watercolour papers which have a texture that is too pronounced and papers that are too heavily coated.

Mouldmade papers made from cotton, such as Fabriano, take watercolour paints well without being too absorbent; they are good for drawing, too. Aquarelle Arches is also excellent for line and wash drawings. Among English papers, Saunders, RWS (Royal Watercolour Society) and Waterford are all of good quality and reasonably inexpensive.

Additionally, I have found some papers which, though not intended for watercolour, can nevertheless yield fine results — a number of print-making or printing papers, for example, are sensitive to the grainy texture of watercolour or gouache.

Watercolour papers are classified by weight and surface texture. Cold-pressed (C.P.), or Not, are most frequently used. Hot-pressed (H.P.) papers have a smoother surface which makes them suitable for fine detail. The "right" side of the paper is determined by the maker's name which appears as a watermark, reading in the right direction.

Lightweight papers — less than 90lb — need to be stretched before you use them with watercolour. Dampen the paper evenly and then secure it to a supporting board with gummed tape around the edges. As the paper dries it should become as tight as a drum. The heavier weights of paper do not require stretching and can be fastened to a support with clips.

Weights and measures

Paper sizes and weights are normally given in metric, but some papers are still measured in Imperial. Weight is measured in grams per square metre (gsm or gm^2) — for example, 100gsm is a light paper, 640gsm is a heavy paper — or in pounds per ream — for example, 72 pounds is a light paper, and 300 pounds is a heavy paper. The following table is a guide to metric and Imperial sizes, which individual makers supply in their own variation of size. "Domestic Etching" paper in the United States is supplied in two sizes: 26 × 40in (66 × 101cm) and 20 × 26in (50 × 66cm).

Metric

A0
841 × 1189mm ($33\frac{1}{8} × 46\frac{3}{4}$in)

A1
594 × 841mm ($23\frac{3}{8} × 33\frac{1}{8}$in)

A2
420 × 594mm ($16\frac{1}{2} × 23\frac{3}{8}$in)

A3
279 × 420mm ($11\frac{3}{4} × 16\frac{1}{2}$in)

A4
210 × 297mm ($8\frac{1}{4} × 11\frac{3}{4}$)

A5
148 × 210mm ($5\frac{7}{8} × 8\frac{1}{4}$in)

Imperial

Antiquarian
53 × 31in (1346 × 787mm)

Double Elephant
40 × $26\frac{1}{4}$in (1016 × 679mm)

Imperial
$30\frac{1}{2} × 22\frac{1}{2}$in (775 × 572mm)

Double Crown
30 × 20in (762 × 508mm)

Royal
24 × 19in (610 × 483mm)

Medium
22 × $17\frac{1}{2}$in (559 × 444mm)

Stretching paper

1 First immerse the entire sheet of paper in cold water and leave for a few minutes to ensure that the moisture is completely absorbed in the fibres of the paper. Lift the sheet and tilt it to remove the excess water from the surface of the paper.

2 Lay the sheet on a drawing board, making sure that there is a wide enough margin all round the paper to tape it down to the board.

3 Using a sponge dampened with water, moisten thoroughly four strips of gummed paper tape.

4 Stick down the paper tape along each edge of the paper. Make sure that the paper is free of wrinkles when secured. Leave the board to dry on a flat surface away from direct heat. If it is left next to a radiator or other source of heat, this might cause the paper to buckle. If possible, leave to dry overnight so that the paper is absolutely dry before you use it.

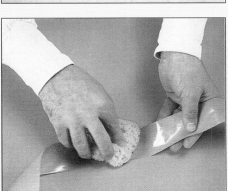

Papers are manufactured in a variety of weights and sizes. They can also be bought in single sheets and pads. Certain papers are made in 10-metre rolls (almost 33ft) which can be cut according to your individual requirements.

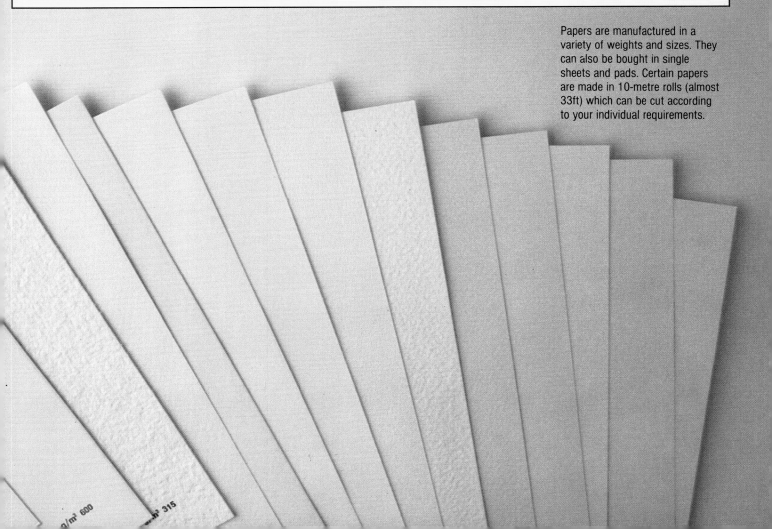

DRAWING TECHNIQUES

To draw "properly" does not mean that you should try to draw like someone
else – nor should you be unduly worried about "style". You should perhaps
begin by asking yourself if you really want to make drawings, or things that
look like drawings.

It may sound obvious to suggest that in order
to produce landscape paintings you must first
learn to see. But nature cannot be interpreted
unless we learn to unlock its secrets by precise
observation. Drawing is the language of the eye
– it is the means by which we gain
understanding of our visual sensations. When
we draw something, we first commit to memory
what we have seen and then transfer each
detail to paper or canvas relating each element
to the next, as if charting our way through
unknown territory.

Before deciding on a particular drawing
technique, there are two things to bear in mind.
First, be sure that you select the technique that
best suits your intentions. If, for instance, you
are concentrating on the solidity of forms in a
landscape, then perhaps charcoal might be
more suitable than a hard pencil. If, on the other
hand, you are tracing the intricate structure of a
building, then a pencil would be better.

The second point to remember is that
nothing should impede the spontaneous
co-ordination between your hand and eye – a
scratchy pen, or a worn brush which won't
allow you to make the marks you want, will
simply cause frustration and block the
development of your drawing or painting.

I drew this sketch of a fisherman's
hut using a 3B graphite pencil, on
Saunders pure rag paper. All the
strokes were made holding the pencil
overhand, although you can use the
pencil underhand, particularly to
make quick, broad marks. There are
many huts on this flat promontory,
but I selected this one as a reference
to use later in a painting.

Sticks of graphite, Black Beauty, and carpenter's flat pencils are useful when you are working on large sheets of paper. Coloured pencils are good for making colour notes, or as a coloured underdrawing to be worked up later into a painting.

Pencil

Pencil is one of the first implements we learn to make a mark with. The most commonly used pencils are graphite pencils, which are graded from very hard to soft. The hard lines of a sharp 6H pencil will be very faint and incisive, whereas a 6B pencil will render soft gradations of tone, from grey to near black. A medium grade such as 2B or 3B will probably be suitable for most purposes. The surface and texture of the paper used can also influence the quality of line.

Other types of pencil include propelling pencils, art pencils, water-soluble pencils and graphite sticks. Unlike pencils, graphite sticks do not need constant sharpening. Extremely soft gradations of tone can be produced with various grades of graphite. As with charcoal, it is best used for making broad statements rather than rendering fine detail. Each type of pencil gives a different type of line and density of tone, so experiment with several kinds to find out the type you feel most comfortable with.

There is perhaps nothing more expressive in art than lines drawn with a pencil. The pressure of the hand on a pencil produces marks of varying quality which reflect your responses to light, weight and texture. It is in drawing that we see most clearly the working of the artist's mind. The lines can be sure or hesitant, suggest delicacy or brute force, convey light and shade, and even hint at colour.

Soft pencils are generally more suitable for landscape drawing than hard ones. They range from B to 8B (the blackest) – a 2B or 3B is suitable for most purposes. Hard pencils range from 9H (the hardest) to HB. They make incisive, pale grey lines and are best used for architectural detail.

B 2B 3B 4B 5B 6B

CHARCOAL

Charcoal, which is made from burnt vine or willow, is the oldest and most natural of drawing media. It is also a very rewarding and delightful medium to work with; it is painterly, being sensitive and precise.

Charcoal is sold in stick form of different widths. You can give it a sharp point by breaking the stem or rubbing the end on some fine sandpaper. Compressed charcoal is made by compressing charcoal powder. It is less brittle but less sensitive than stick charcoal. Compressed charcoal pencils are graded soft, medium and hard.

You can use charcoal to produce a variety of lines, to make bold statements, or a wide range of tones from dark to the most subtle shades. Degas was a master of the charcoal drawing, combining strong contours with great sensitivity.

It is important to be aware of the particular qualities of charcoal — it is no good, for instance, trying to draw fine architectural detail with it. Instead, use it for broader shapes and work on paper large enough to accommodate strokes drawn at arms' length.

Charcoal can be easily modified, corrected or redrawn. Many striking charcoal drawings have been produced where the tones have been smudged a great deal to conceal what is basically a weak underlying drawing.

All charcoal drawings need to be fixed with a fixative. Do this as soon as possible after you complete your drawing, because even the slightest smudge can spoil the clarity of the drawing.

Retreating from the rain on a Swiss lake, I took refuge in the boat station. The iron tracery of the window looking out onto the lake was particularly pretty and gave an unusual appearance to the landscape outside, so I decided to paint the scene. To retain the delicacy of the ironwork and at the same time hint at its iron-grey colour, I chose to draw just its outlines, in charcoal. The soft, smudgy quality of charcoal was appropriate for the softness of this landscape. Having defined the space of the composition with the charcoal drawing, I then laid in patches of watercolour. I finished off the work by smudging areas of charcoal to suggest the smoke billowing from the funnel of the steamboat, and gave the pale grey area on the right more depth with some pencil shading.

Right: Charcoal doesn't have to be restricted to sketches or outlines, as this image of a park shows. It has been applied densely in some areas which contrast sharply with the light areas, some of which are untouched. Solid black lines hold the composition together; the over-all effect is highly atmospheric.

In this landscape in Tuscany (**below**), I used the charcoal stick with exuberant short and long strokes to hint at the foliage of the olive tree in the foreground and suggest the dark conical masses of cypress trees in the background. By varying the strokes I created a highly patterned effect. The result hints at colour, even though none is used.

Twig charcoal looks different from compressed sticks in that it has a slightly curved and sometimes knobbly appearance, whereas compressed sticks are straight and uniform in shape.

PASTELS

Pastels are frequently associated with pretty, insipid hues, but their colours are actually so vivid that the difficulty is often how to tone them down. When visiting Degas one day, Vollard heard him say "What a devil of a job it is to bleach the colour out of pastel crayons! I soak them over and over again, and even put them in the sun . . .", and people still thought he had them made specially to achieve such a brilliant colour!

Pastels are useful in that they are easy to carry around and so enable you to produce a work on the spot. They are also a very expressive medium which can be used with great exuberance to create movement in an image. The colours the artist used here are limited, probably because the light was fading. They are predominantly purple and grey, with yellow ochres confined to the buildings. White chalk has been laid over the dark colours of the sky to reintroduce light. The result has a good tonal unity. This image was made with chalk pastels on a heavily grained paper.

There are several kinds of pastel available today. Soft, or chalk, pastels are made from coloured pigment bound with gum and white filler. They are lovely to use in that the colours always appear fresh and opaque. However, they crumble easily and are difficult to control. Oil pastels are very different in character in that they are softer and richer in colour. Hard pastels are like hard chalk and are easy to control, but don't have the intensity of colour or textural quality that soft and oil pastels do.

There are more than 500 tints of pastel, made by varying the proportion of white filler that is added to the pure colour pigment. Such a vast range can be daunting, but you could start with a basic palette of black, blue (ultramarine, cobalt or Prussian blue), white, red (cadmium, alizarin, vermilion or light red), brown (raw umber or burnt sienna), yellow (lemon yellow, yellow ochre, raw sienna or cadmium yellow) and a green, such as terre verte or viridian.

The choice of paper support for pastel is quite important. Toned papers, such as Ingres or Canson Mi-Teintes, have sufficient "tooth" to hold the chalk.

One of the first things to realize about pastel is that, unlike oil, watercolour or gouache, you mix and blend the colours as part of the drawing process. Mixing colour on the surface of the paper can be difficult. I would recommend starting to draw with black, white, and two or three colours on a toned paper, before attempting to use a wider range of colour. In this way you learn to sort out the drawing tonally, without being confused by too many competing colours.

If you are working on a tinted paper, you will be imposing light as well as dark parts of the drawing on a neutral ground and will need to bear this in mind when you plan your colours.

With soft or chalk pastels, any unwanted parts of the drawing can usually be brushed away with a hog's-hair brush. With oil pastels, once you have applied the pastel to paper, you can thin the pigment with turpentine or white mineral spirit.

Pastel can be successfully combined with other media such as gouache or tempera. It is possible to produce a thin underpainting with gouache before working over it with pastel.

Fixing your drawing in stages may be necessary where one part of the drawing needs to be preserved before you go on to the next stage. Most pastel drawings need to be fixed anyway, after they are completed, so that the pigment does not drop off the paper. A mouth spray diffuser is preferable to aerosol fixatives.

Soft, or chalk pastels, are altogether more subtle than oil, and when blended cannot be corrected easily. But you should not be afraid to push the medium as far as possible in order to gain a better understanding of what colour mixtures can be achieved. Experiment on a spare sheet of paper until you become more confident.

The smoothness of oil pastels lends itself well to blending, and the mixture of different colours on the paper's surface can suggest further ideas. The pigment can also be burnished with a fingertip or torchon (paper stump) and is easily scraped off again with a knife if the colour is unsatisfactory.

PEN AND INK

Pen and ink is often underrated as a medium for landscapes, but it has been used with great success by the Old Masters: with a few strokes of a reed pen, Rembrandt was able to establish a whole landscape; Van Gogh employed the thick and thin strokes of a pen to create a wealth of rhythmic lines in his landscape drawings; and Turner sometimes combined pen and red ink with watercolour.

I drew this image very rapidly, using a dip pen and Indian ink. Pen and ink is a good medium for scenes where buildings predominate because it conveys the hard horizontal and vertical lines of architecture well. To relieve the static quality of the drawing. I spattered some ink onto the sky area with a toothbrush and created some movement in the foreground by sketching the grass loosely, with curving strokes.

Pens can be as simple as sharpened bamboo or a stick, onto which you fit a variety of metal nibs, or as sophisticated as a fibre-tipped pen, a ball pen, or a fountain pen. Each has its own characteristic quality of line.

There are a number of types of pen you can use, from technical pens, felt-tipped pens and ball-point, to bamboo, reed, quill, and even cow parsley stalks.

Many pens have metal nibs, which are produced in a variety of shapes from fine points to broad chisel shapes. Some pens can be fitted with brass reservoirs to retain more ink. Reed and quill pens, which preceded the metal nib, produce a softer, more irregular line. The quality of this line relates directly to the way that the reed or quill has been cut. Felt- or plastic-tipped pens are now increasingly being used for drawing directly from landscape subjects. The fluent line they produce makes them ideal for working rapidly from observation without the bother of having to continually dip the pen into a pot of ink. The broader tipped pens are

remarkably like reed pens in shape and performance. Their only disadvantage, perhaps, is that unlike pens with metal nibs, there is less variety in the quality of line they produce. These pens are filled with water- or spirit-based inks which can be blended with water or turpentine respectively.

You can use watercolour, and Chinese and Indian inks for drawing, although Indian ink clogs conventional fountain pens because it is waterproof. However, there are now pens available which are suitable for Indian ink. The watercolour inks manufactured today are based on modern synthetic and organic pigments with a high degree of permanence. They are particularly useful in paintings where a richer concentration of colour is required. If, for instance, your subject demands strongly

contrasted colours, then coloured inks combined with dry watercolours would be suitable.

Try drawing different marks on a few trial sheets of paper to discover the richness and variety of lines you can produce, this will give you more confidence to work more fluently.

The first requisite of pen drawing is to make sure that you know what you want to do before you begin drawing, because the quality of line needs to be sustained throughout and mistakes are not easily remedied. The best policy is to have a quantity of thin, inexpensive paper (preferably with a smooth surface), so that you can try out your drawing a number of times. Try to draw by exploiting the particular qualities of line that are given by the nib you are using. Allow the line to work without adding laborious cross-hatching.

Transparent coloured inks are good for laying over a black line drawing. They work well, too, as an underdrawing for a painting in watercolour.

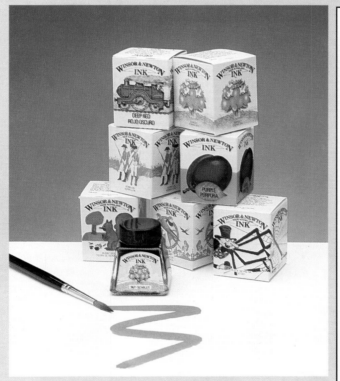

Making a reed pen

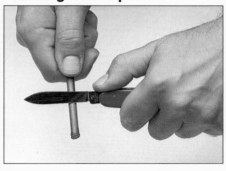

1 With a sharp knife, trim a reed or a stick of bamboo, until you have a sharp point.

2 By pushing the reed away from you on the paper, or pulling it towards you, you can create quite different strokes.

From left to right, the first mark was drawn with a fibre-tipped pen, the next three with a dip pen with different nibs, followed by a fountain pen, a reed pen, a bamboo stick and another reed pen.

For this drawing of Dorset Harbour I chose a vertical format, to emphasize the sense of distance in the composition. Using a pen and brush on soft cartridge/drawing paper, I deliberately made the brush line softer, to contrast with the more linear elements of the drawing. I made some areas solid to strengthen the main shapes and to balance the drawing tonally. To give additional texture to the rocks, I stippled ink onto them with a sponge.

I made this little drawing of the Basilica of St Francis in Assisi using pen and Indian ink. The black and white of the medium suited the harsh contrasts of light and shade in the brightness of the day. So as not to detract from the simplicity of the horizontal and vertical lines, I decided to shade the dark areas with vertical lines rather than with cross-hatching. To break up the stark whiteness of the sky, I spattered some ink onto it with a toothbrush.

Above: the pattern of the bands of repeated windows and the wheel of the paddle on this steamboat appealed to me, and I felt that it would look best drawn in simple outline. I drew the boat directly onto Arches paper with a reed pen and black waterproof ink. The column of the tree trunk helps to break up the entirely horizontal character of the boat, and the funnel, emphasized with a solid black area, provides a strong focal point in what would otherwise be a very delicate drawing.

Left: this drawing was done as an illustration for a hand-printed book on the myth of Daphnis and Chloe. Because there was no colour in the book, pen and ink was an appropriate medium. I used an old-fashioned fountain pen with a broad nib bought for a few pence in a junk shop. The girl posed for me, and I then added the landscape elements, which are symbols in the myth.

DRAWING FOR PAINTING

Drawings can be done for three purposes, to be a finished work in themselves, as reference for a later work, or as the basis for a painting.

There are a number of reasons why it is sometimes necessary to use working drawings as reference for landscape paintings produced in the studio. An artist travelling through a country, for instance, may not have sufficient time to develop a painting directly from observation. Turner, on his journeys down the Rhine, made colour notes at the end of each day from simple outline pencil drawings which aided his memory. Other artists actually prefer to work away from the subject: Bonnard, for example, said that he felt intimidated in front of the motif; he preferred to work from drawings and the colours and hues he had committed to memory. The memory plays an important part, for, no matter how exact the drawing is, you need to be able to remember how a place looked under certain conditions of light.

The kind of drawings that you use for reference are not intended for exhibition, though they are often interesting. What matters most is

Above: this scene appealed to me because the structure bearing the overhead electric cable relates well to the main proportions of the church. With the intention of working the drawing up at a later date, I made sure that it carried sufficient information to remind me of the original scene. However, I should have made notes of the colours if I wanted to work it up into a painting, because I would not be able to remember them exactly later on.

Left: the half-round wooden eaves that overhang the "Rose" house, in Altishofen, Switzerland, are characteristic of farmhouses in Canton Luzern. I liked it because the light pink stucco made a pleasing contrast with the faded bottle-green of the wood. I quickly drew an outline of the building in pencil to make a note of the structure, and then laid in patches of colour as an aide-memoire.

that your drawing should have sufficient information from which you can develop a convincing painting. Some artists use a kind of shorthand to make notes of colours and tones. If, for example, you remember a patch of colour looking like burnt chocolate, you might make a note to that effect. It is also useful to note whether a colour is warm or cool.

The drawing done "sight-size", that is to say the size we draw naturally, may need to be enlarged if you are going to paint on canvas. Cover your drawing with a transparent grid of horizontal and vertical lines; repeat the grid on your canvas (adjusting the scale to the size of your canvas), and transfer the image square by square. If a drawing is squared-up in this way, it is important to try and maintain the spontaneity of the original.

Left: small chapels such as this are a feature of certain cantons in Switzerland and punctuate the landscape in an interesting way. Local people were curious to see an Englishman drawing such a simple building while at the same time ignoring the Schloss that was the pride of the village. Children circled round me on their bicycles, making it very difficult to concentrate, especially while working in a cold wind. I made the original sketch in pencil and watercolour in early spring, when the colour was still bleached by several months of snow.

Left: I developed this oil painting in the studio from the watercolour sketch above. Tonally it is stronger than the sketch, but I resisted the temptation to overwork the detail. The composition is based on the relationship of a few simple elements, with the single vertical pole dividing the picture at a point roughly in relation to the Golden Section.

SKETCHBOOKS

Sketchbooks are immensely useful as a ready means of making visual notes, because they are easily portable and can just be whisked out of a pocket or bag when you see something you want to record. They are also useful for keeping reference pictures together. Sketchbooks, like diaries, are an intimate record of an artist's progress over the years; I still have sketchbooks that I produced when I was twelve or thirteen years old.

Sketchbooks are manufactured in a great many shapes and sizes; many conform to the "A" series, from A1 to A5 ($22\frac{3}{8} \times 33\frac{1}{8}$in to $5\frac{7}{8} \times 8\frac{1}{4}$in), which is not always suitable proportionally. Pocket sketchbooks (A5) are particularly useful for journeys and for exploring ideas for composition.

The quality of paper ranges from thin, inexpensive cartridge (drawing paper) to heavier weights of watercolour paper. I generally prefer a sketchbook with a spiral binding, because the pages can be folded back easily for drawing.

The main disadvantage of a sketchbook, to my mind, is its uniformity of size. I prefer to select my own paper as single sheets and cut them to various sizes, which I keep sandwiched between two stout sheets of thick cardboard with clips. The board makes an ideal support when working outside, and the clips prevent the paper from blowing about too much.

Sketchbooks provide a record of the working of an artist's first ideas in response to things seen. They also chart his or her particular interests, obsessions and discoveries.

BRUSHES

Good-quality brushes should be the first priority for any landscape painter. It is difficult and frustrating to work with inferior brushes which will not make the kind of mark you require. Though expensive, good brushes, when looked after properly, can be a painter's best friend.

A good brush will hold its shape and retain its springiness while you are working. Brushes made from synthetic materials do not generally hold their shape as well as those made with natural bristles, though more recently the quality of synthetics has improved considerably.

Watercolour brushes have a short handle and are held like a pencil. Oil painting brushes have longer handles and are usually held at arm's length. For watercolour I generally use sable brushes in sizes 3 to 6 for detail, and squirrel or ox-hair brushes for laying washes. For oil painting I use sable brushes for drawing and hog's hair for laying-in colour.

Brushes are cut to different shapes for producing fine and broad brushstrokes. "Round" brushes are used for watercolour and for fine detail in oil painting. Short-bristled brushes with a chisel edge are called "brights". They are useful for covering large areas of canvas or paper with colour. "Filbert" brushes also have short bristles, but the edge is curved for producing a broad line. All brushes are made in a range of sizes.

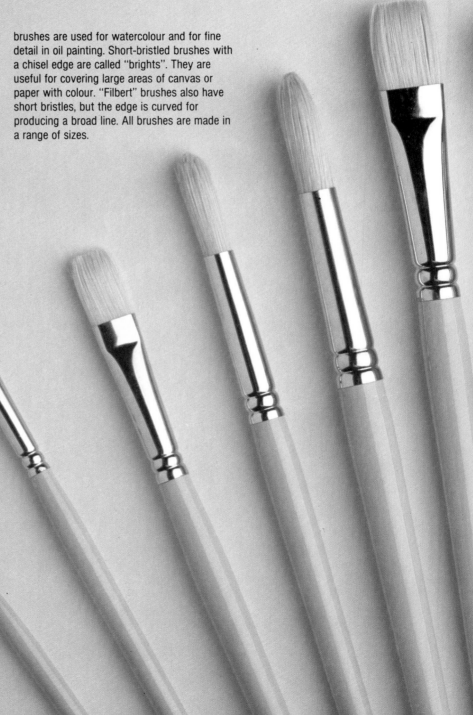

Among the large range of brushes available, the best are hog's hair (the pale-bristled brushes on the left), ox hair (in the centre) and sable (the light brown brushes on the right). Hog's hair are best for oil and sable for watercolour, although both can be used for either medium. The broad flat and fan-shaped hog's hair brushes are best for laying washes.

Brushes will last a long time if they are cleaned after use and handled correctly. A sable brush, for instance, will soon be ruined if it is used to scrub paint over the surface. Wash watercolour brushes gently in soap and warm water until all trace of colour has gone, squeeze the hair dry, and reshape it with your thumb and forefinger. Soak oil painting brushes in turpentine and then wash them in soap and water as above.

The connection between artist and brush is a personal one. The popular image of an artist's studio with pots of brushes belies the fact that most artists generally make use of a few brushes which have been worn into a particular shape and are like trusted friends. Try out a few of the many types to find out which suits your needs best.

WATERCOLOUR

Watercolour is an ideal medium for working directly from landscape subjects because it dries quickly and the few materials required to use it are easily packed into a small shoulder bag. Watercolour is basically pigment bound in water-soluble gum arabic. When a brush loaded with water thins the gum, a transparent wash of colour can be produced on paper. It is the translucence of the coloured washes that distinguishes watercolour from other media.

Choosing watercolour paints

Watercolours can be bought as a pre-selected range of colours in the form of semi-moist cakes or pans, contained in a metal box. Half-pans are small square cakes of colour and are the most readily available. If, however, you intend to work on fairly large sheets of paper, the larger pans are more useful because they enable you to mix a sufficient quantity of paint to lay a large area of wash.

Alternatively, tubes of colour or bottles of watercolour inks can be bought individually. My own preference is to buy an empty box and fill it with my choice of cakes of colours, and to have as a standby tubes of the colours that I use most frequently. When working on location it is essential that nothing gets in the way while you are concentrating on the subject you are painting. For this reason I prefer a box with fixed cakes of paint because I can use the lid of the box as a mixing palette. However, there are now some ingeniously designed boxes which have their own fold-out water containers.

There are two grades of colour — artist's and student's — but in my experience the student grades simply do not provide the richness of colour obtainable with the professional range. Look carefully at the description of the paints when buying: most manufacturers give clear guidance as to the permanence or fugitiveness of their colours.

The choice of a colour palette is a personal matter, but a range of twelve colours should meet most of your needs. A basic range for landscape painting might be composed of the following: cadmium yellow, yellow ochre, burnt sienna, burnt umber, alizarin crimson, cadmium red, Indian red, Payne's grey, cerulean blue, ultramarine, Monastral blue, and lamp black.

The preliminary stages

The success or failure of a watercolour is dependant, to some extent, on the kind of decisions made before the painting begins; unlike oil paint, watercolour cannot be scraped or scrubbed too much because its translucence

This palette of twelve colours should meet most requirements for landscape and seascape painting. Additionally a tube of white gouache might prove useful should you wish to combine washes of transparent colour with semi-opaque tints of colour. Turner sometimes added opaque white to heighten lighter passages of his paintings. With experience you will no doubt develop a predilection for certain colour combinations.

Try laying one transparent wash of colour over another to produce a further colour; sometimes the results you get will be quite unexpected.

It helps to plan your watercolour before you actually apply the paint. A drawing is particularly useful in this respect because it establishes a structure that you can use as a guide when painting, and also helps to determine the area of the washes when you come to lay them. This drawing can be restated with a fine brush to become part of the finished work, as in these images of boats on the water.

and clarity of colour are destroyed. This is why a preliminary drawing is helpful. However, a drawing will show through a wash in every detail, which means that it is easy for the drawing to dominate the final work. Early topographical studies of the English landscape, for example, were little more than tinted drawings. It is important to achieve a balance between line and wash. In the watercolours of Cézanne, for instance, neither line nor wash is subordinate to each other and the balance between the two produces a vibrant harmony.

As an alternative to pencil you might use a brush or pen to create the main structure of the drawing. The choice depends on the subject, however. If, for example, I am drawing a building, such as a Palladian church in Venice, I usually work with pencil before I begin to establish tones with watercolour. If, on the other hand I am confronted with an atmospheric scene of mountains and lakes, I might begin drawing straight away with a brush.

Laying washes

1 Dampen the stretched paper and make sure you have enough of your chosen colour ready-mixed. Tilt the board forward slightly, and work from left to right, then apply the next strip of colour from right to left. Continue in this way.

2 Each band of paint you apply should overlap the previous one, to pick up excess paint and allow the edges of each band to blend with the next, and so that you achieve a flat, uniform wash.

To create a gradated wash of colour, lay each band of colour while the one before it is still wet. You can do this either with the same colour, diluting it further for each successive band, or with different colours.

Left: for a more varied effect, rub over the paper with a white wax candle, where you want areas to remain white. The wax will resist any washes you paint over it.

Right: to produce a pastel-like, thicker appearance, add starch powder to your paint. This technique was used by nineteenth-century English watercolourists.

Handling watercolour

In a temperate climate, the subtle continuous changes of colour and tones can be rendered more readily in watercolour because it is so spontaneous. Gradations of tone and colour can be achieved by varying the strength of the wash and also by superimposing a wash of one colour over another. However, the most successful watercolours are usually those that employ no more than three or four separate washes, because the transparency and clarity of the colour are lost when too many washes are used. Always work in terms of the medium, trying to retain the transparency of the wash. If it is used with insufficient water, the paint will be as opaque as gouache.

In general, work from light to dark. In landscape, where the sky is often the palest and purest colour, work from top to bottom. There are practical reasons for doing this — it is difficult to achieve pale sky tints after the water has become muddied with earth tints such as burnt umber.

There are a number of watercolour techniques, such as applying colour wet-on-wet, but these are hazardous and difficult to control, and it seems pointless to create problems unnecessarily. Turner, it is claimed, said that some of his best watercolours were produced by suspending the painting in a water barrel. But then he knew exactly what he was doing! The subject itself should determine the way it is treated technically.

Laying a wash

Apart from defining a structure, a preliminary drawing also helps to determine the main areas where washes are to be laid on the paper. But do not apply this too vigorously — many paintings fail because the various coloured washes are confined to specific parts of the composition. Think of how you might extend the blue or grey wash used for a sky, for instance, to shadows on buildings, foliage and grass. Use a wash as an undertone so that in the final painting it appears in the original hue on white areas of paper but also underpins and influences colours elsewhere in the painting. This creates a unity throughout the work. The watercolours of Cézanne demonstrate this admirably.

Have in mind the kind of shape the wash is going to make before you actually lay it and make sure that the brush is of the right size for the area to be covered. Control the flow of the wash with the tip of the brush and do not tilt the paper too steeply. A wash or a brushstroke dries with a softer edge when the paper is slightly damp, and with a harder edge on a dry surface.

After laying a wash I usually squeeze the remaining moisture from the brush and use it to absorb any surplus liquid at the bottom edge of the wash. As a general rule, it is always a good idea to mix more colour than you will actually need. An old plate or saucer might be more useful for this than a small ceramic palette.

Once a wash has been laid, don't be tempted to move it around. Allow it to settle and dry, and let the rich grainy gradations of pigment become anchored to the surface of the paper as the water evaporates. Get to know what happens when coloured washes are superimposed over one another, and also practise mixing colours on scraps of paper.

GOUACHE

Gouache is, in my view, much underrated as a medium for landscape painting. It is used exactly like watercolour, except that it is opaque. This opaque quality makes gouache better suited to subjects where rich, solid colours are wanted, rather than the more delicate tints of watercolour, as in an autumnal scene, for example. It also means that gouache can be used on toned papers.

Sometimes called "body colour", gouache is made from pigment ground with white filler and bound in gum. Being water-soluble, it can be applied thinly, as a wash, which will be more granular than watercolour, or it can be laid as a thick impasto.

The range of colours is extensive. The colours have great permanence and are less likely to fade than watercolours. When using them, remember that the colour dries lighter than when first applied.

Gouache can be applied to almost any support, including watercolour paper and cardboard. Watercolour and gouache can be combined successfully, especially in landscape, where there is a need for both translucent washes of colour and stronger, more solid, earth colours.

Unlike watercolour, you are less likely to be sidetracked by clever techniques when using gouache. However, try to exploit the dryness of the medium. The gouache paintings of Edouard Vuillard, for example, make use of the chalkiness of the medium, giving it no gloss or transparency.

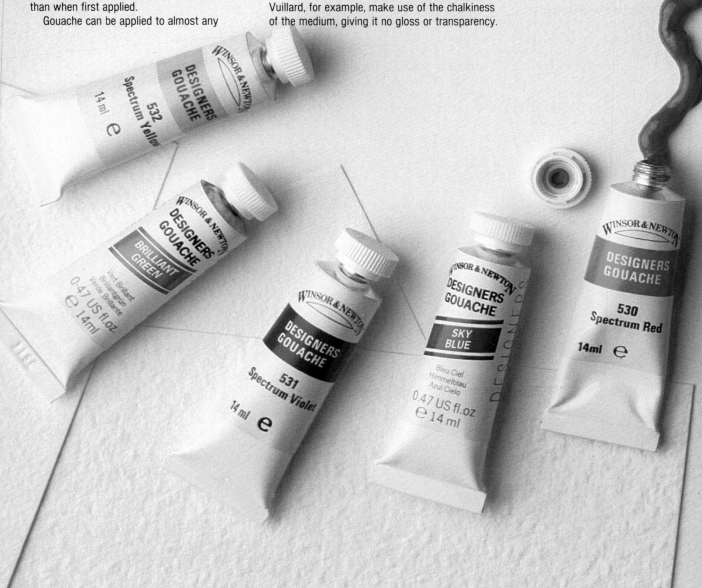

Above: looking closely at the scrubland of the image on the right, you can see how I applied the earth colours, blending transparent washes with thickly applied paint. The washes were laid first, and allowed to dry before being overlaid with thicker paint.

Right: gouache seemed the ideal medium for this subject because of the positive colours of the scene — the black tarred hut, the reds of the earth, and the graphic contrast of the white window frames. The fishing hut is situated on a bleak promontory of reclaimed land and I deliberately included a large amount of foreground to emphasize its barrenness, desolation and flatness.

Left: I painted this field in Devon on cardboard primed with gesso. The rich red earth relating to the green hedgerow attracted me, as well as the thin stretch of sea just visible in the distance. The single row of telegraph poles receding into the distance helps to define the perspective of the image; this is further enhanced by the extent of foreground, which exaggerates the sense of space.

Right: this detail of the hut above reveals the greasy black crayon used to give shape and texture to the drawing under the wash. The crayon resists the paint to some extent, resulting in a gritty appearance.

SUPPORTS

The material that we paint on is called a "support". There are various materials which can be used, but it is important to use the right support for the medium you choose. Paper, cardboard, canvas, hardboard (masonite), wood and metal are all supports.

Some supports have a "ground", which is a coating applied either by the artist or the manufacturer to provide a suitably textured surface to work on. A support must be "primed" if you want it to be non-absorbent – this is particularly important when using oil paints. An unprimed canvas will absorb oil from the pigment, leaving an image on the surface which may be far removed from what was originally intended.

Stretched canvas is the traditional support for oil painting. Not only is it extremely durable, but the "tooth" of the material makes it an ideal surface to work on. Fine and coarse weaves of linen are generally used, though cotton duck is a suitable alternative. Prepared canvas can be bought ready-stretched, or you may prefer to stretch and prime it yourself.

There are a great many recipes for the preparation of painting supports. Much depends on whether or not you are the kind of person who enjoys being involved in the craft of preparing materials. If you are impatient to be out working, then you might find it easier to buy what you require "off the shelf".

If you want to stretch canvas, standard sizes of wooden slats with morticed corners are available and easily assembled into a frame for the canvas. Cut the canvas with an overlap, and staple or tack one edge to the centre of one side of a wooden frame. Stretch the canvas and tack it from the opposite side. Continue until all the sides are evenly stretched. Stretchers are sold with small wooden wedges which, when tapped into each slotted corner, provide additional tension to the canvas.

Priming is done in two stages. First, size the canvas with rabbit size (available from artists' materials suppliers). Size is made from one part rabbit-skin glue, to fifteen parts water. Blend the size over a stove and apply it to the canvas while still warm. Then, when dry, give the canvas at least two coats of primer. The primer can be mixed from one part linseed oil and flake white powder, to six parts turpentine. Blend the turpentine and oil together and then add the flake white to make a chalky mixture. Allow each coat of primer to dry thoroughly before applying the next.

Size and primer can be used for other supports. Hardboard (masonite) is inexpensive and can be bought from most hardware stores. Make sure that you use the smooth side of the board, but first sand it lightly to give the surface some tooth. Cardboard and plywood are also suitable supports. In fact, most surfaces will do. Hilaire Hiler, in his book *Notes on the Technique of Painting* (1934), relates that one of Gauguin's most technically sound paintings was done on an old door panel! Toulouse-Lautrec, too, frequently used offcuts of old strawboard, or brown cardboard, for some of his best paintings.

A support is, literally, anything you paint or draw on. Traditionally, paintings are done on canvas. You can buy this ready-stretched and primed, in a variety of sizes, or if you prefer you can buy a frame and a roll of canvas and stretch and prime it yourself.

OIL AND ACRYLIC

There is something about the process of painting in oil which defies description. It is as if the difficulties encountered in themselves suggest further ideas – the more one uses oil paint, the more one discovers a way forward. Acrylic presents a suitable alternative to oil.

When we look at the early oil paintings of Van Gogh, there is none of the thick expressive strokes of paint that characterize his later work. In Cézanne's oil paintings, we can trace the evolution of his technique from a heavy impasto to much thinner, narrow brush strokes in his late landscapes. It is almost as if development is part of the nature of the medium. Perhaps this is why it is still the medium most widely used by artists.

Oil paints are manufactured by mixing coloured pigments with vegetable oils such as poppy or linseed oil. Constable and other landscape painters in the eighteenth century used oil paints from skin bladders, so that they could work in the open air, directly from nature. Today, oil paint is manufactured in tubes and tins, in two grades: artist's quality, and student's grade (which is less permanent).

Once on the canvas, the drying process of oils is slow, and varies according to temperature, humidity, and the proportion of oil used in relation to pigment. The slow drying of the medium is a distinct advantage when working on a painting over a period of time. Even when dry, the colours do not change in their tonality.

By using varying proportions of linseed oil and turpentine mixed with the paint, you can work from transparent glazes to a thicker, almost sculptural impasto.

As an exercise in mixing oil paint, I would recommend the following: first divide your tubes of colours into warm and cool colours. Make sure that you have a large tube of white. Using only white and black, see how many warm greys you can mix on one palette, and on a second palette, how many cool greys you can produce. Then try working on a painting from a reference drawing, using a harmony of warm and cool greys. This exercise will help you to get out of the habit of relying on ready-mixed

Left: acrylic paint can be used in a heavy impasto, so that it resembles oil paint and can be applied with a palette knife. It can also be thinned to resemble gouache or tempera and laid on with a brush. It is an extremely versatile medium with a great degree of permanence. The main advantage it has over oil is the rapidity with which it dries.

Right: when using oil paint, it is best to apply it thinly in the preliminary stages of a painting, and then to thicken the coat of each superimposed layer progressively. Working from thin to thick assists the drying considerably.

colours and will also teach you a great deal about colour harmony.

Most artists begin by making an underpainting or drawing on the canvas. Then, when the main structure has been established, the larger areas of colour can be blocked in and related to one another.

Acrylic

Acrylic paints provide the landscape artist with a very flexible medium. They are diluted with water, dry rapidly, and adhere firmly to almost any kind of support.

In surface texture, the matt quality of acrylic is closer to gouache or tempera than to oil paint. Its covering capacity makes it ideal for large canvases.

Acrylic paints can be used in fine transparent glazes when thinned with water. Alternatively, colours can be mixed without further thinning to achieve an impasto effect. Additives can be mixed with the paint to make it even thicker. Much depends on what you are trying to achieve. The versatility of the medium has converted many artists who previously worked in oil, though, in my view, an oil-bound pigment makes the colour richer in tone.

EASELS

Easels are not absolutely essential when you are painting – you may actually
prefer working on the kitchen table, or if you are working outside, drawing
frequently from observation, you might find an easel too cumbersome.
Only experience can help you judge just how useful an easel might be.

What posture do you normally adopt when you
are painting? Do you, for instance, prefer to
remain on your feet and occasionally stand
back from your work? If so, an easel might be
useful. If, on the other hand, you prefer to
spread your work out on a flat surface, then a
trestle table will be just as good as an easel.

There are folding easels which are easily
carried outside, but in my experience the less
you have to carry the more energy you will have
for your drawing.

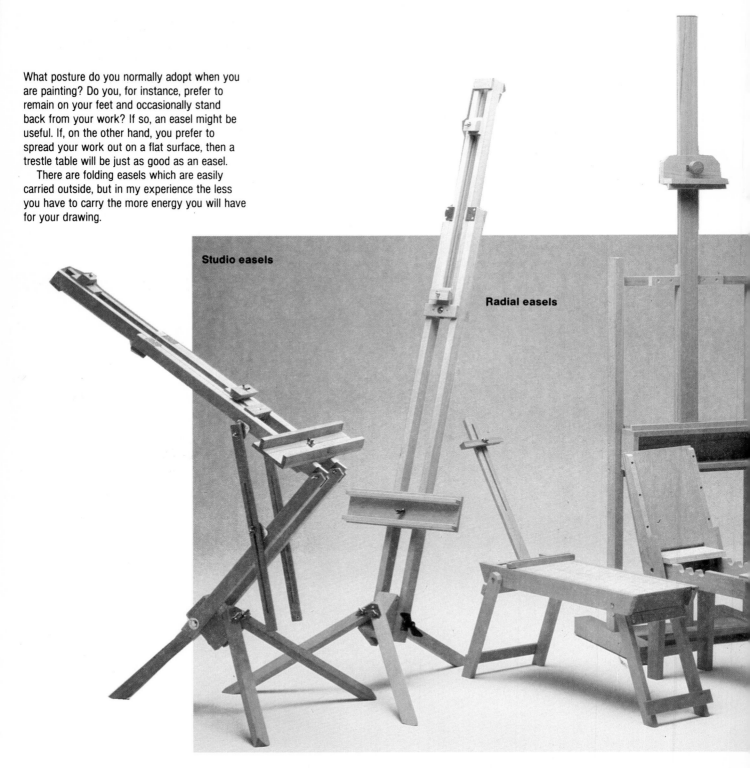

Studio easels

Radial easels

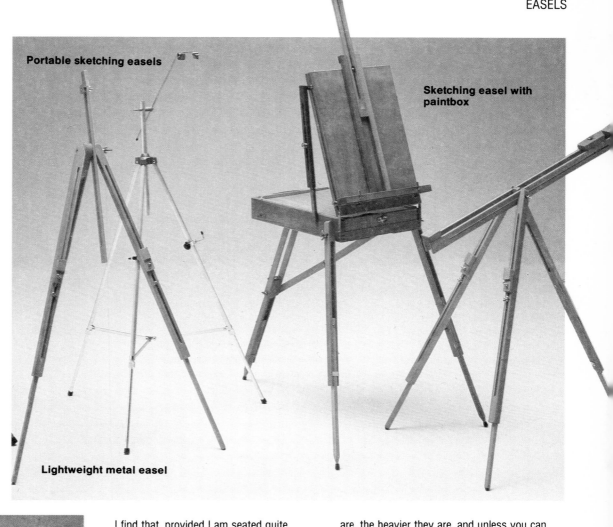

Portable sketching easels

Sketching easel with paintbox

Portable sketching stool

Lightweight metal easel

Artist's donkeys

I find that, provided I am seated quite comfortably, I don't mind balancing my board and paper on my knees. However, if you need to work from observation over a long period of time you might find an easel invaluable. The kind of easel that you would use outside would need to be fairly robust to stand up to windy conditions — some artists use the kind of guy ropes that are used on tents so that the easel can be pegged firmly to the ground. If you feel that an easel would be of definite advantage, then it is worthwhile asking your art supplier if you can test several types for lightness, ease of assembly and so on.

Most manufacturers produce portable sketching easels in wood and metal. They generally have telescopic legs so that the height of the easel can be adjusted to enable you to work standing or sitting down. There are some easels which are incorporated into a paintbox; another combines a seat and easel and is called an artist's donkey. The more complicated they

are, the heavier they are, and unless you can load everything into a car or work quite close to home, then such an easel will simply become a burden to you.

If you are going to be working in watercolour the easel must allow the drawing board to swing into a horizontal position, otherwise the washes will run out of control down the paper.

Studio easels range from small table-top easels to heavy easels on wheels. I bought my own easel in a furniture sale where one can usually obtain them at a much lower price.

Table-top easels made from wood or aluminium are useful mainly for small watercolours or gouache paintings. Artist's donkeys are mainly used for figure drawing. The most popular easel is the "studio radial", of the type used in life classes at art college: it is robust yet flexible — the central joint allows the easel to be tilted at different angles forwards or backwards. These easels will last a lifetime and they are a good investment.

COLOUR

In nature, most things partly absorb or reflect light and some surfaces partly refract light. The colour of an object is dependent on the intensity of the light rays that it reflects or absorbs. The painter is really concerned with an approximation of colour within the limited means at his or her disposal.

It is eight o'clock on a cloudless April morning. There is a pellucid haze which reduces the distant hills to a single tone of grey-blue. The old tiled roofs of the farm buildings in the foreground are a dusky grey-brown. By midday the same scene will be transformed completely: the hills will become a lush green and previously unseen forms will be revealed. The tiled roofs will radiate with a bright pink-orange glow. The specific, or "local", colour of the roof tiles may be red but, like all colours, it is modified by light.

Sir Isaac Newton (1642–1727)

demonstrated that although sunlight, or white light, is "uncoloured" it is made up of seven coloured rays: violet, indigo, green, blue, yellow, orange and red. We see colour in objects that reflect and absorb these rays to a greater or lesser degree.

An object which reflected the rays completely would be white or uncoloured. If that same object absorbed the same rays, it would look black. "Refracted" light relates to the phenomenon of light passing through a transparent or semi-transparent body; the light is then redirected, or refracted.

Colour in nature is a harmony of contrasts — light against dark, one complementary against another, such as red against green. At the same time, every object has its own, unique colour. While a basic knowledge of colour theory is useful in landscape painting, the time spent observing colour in nature is even more rewarding. You will see colour better if you can stop thinking about the things you know in theory.

Right: at harvest time on this chalky landscape, the colour of the ripe corn enriches the normally neutral tints. The colour range is restricted because of the time of the year; they are mostly earth colours, with some white body colour used in the sky. I also used a toned paper for this image.

Below right: this part of Switzerland, known as the "Napf", is not mountainous but consists mainly of a series of undulating hills with isolated farms and pine forests. This painting was drawn entirely with a brush, and to achieve the misty quality in the background, I applied the colours wet-on-wet. The strong contrast between the middle distance and the background is exaggerated by defining the trees with a black green and diluting the purple of the hills in the distance.

Far left: apart from a few preliminary marks in pencil, the drawing is done with a brush, working rapidly in the strong Tuscan sunlight. The main colours I used were grey, viridian and ochre. To capture the silvery grey of the olive trees, I added opaque white to the viridian. For the olive greens, I got a better colour by mixing yellow with lamp black rather than blue.

Left: this work was painted on a toned paper to avoid the glare of sunlight. The colours are high key and there is little shadow, which reflects the intensity of the midday light. To achieve the pale, washed-out quality of the colours, I added white body colour to all of them. This made the ochres, for example, almost pink.

Colour palette

A simple palette of eight to ten colours is enough for most purposes when working directly from nature. Try to select colours which are appropriate to your subject. If you are producing a series of seascapes, for instance, you might want to include a few additional blues or greens; conversely, if you are painting a landscape in central Italy, you might be frustrated without a tube of ochre or burnt umber.

Buying tubes of the brightest reds, blues and yellows will not turn you into a colourist. If you are painting a landscape for the first time, try seeing how much you can achieve with just two or three colours and with experience you will eventually select a range of colours which relate directly to your needs.

APPROACHING
THE SUBJECT

When we walk through the countryside everything beckons our attention, but sometimes something in particular will correspond to our innermost feelings about the character of a place. Perhaps it has something to do with the relationship of parts, the way that the various elements in a landscape are linked together. When choosing a subject, be selective, deal with one aspect at a time. Begin with the places you know best. If your senses have been dulled by over-familiarity, then plan a journey to somewhere you have not been before. It's a tall order, but you should try to look beyond the picturesque, to uncover those things that you see but do not truly understand. If you draw or paint only those things you can readily identify, your work will be full of clichés.

In the following section you will find several landscapes approached in different ways. I explain them step by step so that you can see how they were achieved, and perhaps be inspired to try some new approaches to your own painting.

COMPOSITION

The word composition has off-putting connotations, suggesting some fearful mathematical formulae which have somehow to be grasped. I prefer to think of composition as visual judgement – knowing by instinct where to place things in the right order.

Landscape is undoubtedly the most popular subject for painters, yet it is also potentially the most difficult to handle in terms of composition. Because landscape is random and orderless, you need a strong sense of design to be able to select and set down the various components of a landscape view which are positioned at different levels and recede into the distance. As a landscape painter you have an advantage over the photographer, in that you can leave out any extraneous detail which intrudes into the general balance of the composition. You control the scene you produce. Turner, for example, sometimes exaggerated the scale of hills and mountains to add greater drama to his work.

The process of composing starts the moment you select a particular viewpoint and before any marks have been made on paper. But it is important to have an awareness of the relationship between the various components of your drawing.

Things are never isolated, but are relative. A single feature might hold your attention – perhaps an isolated white cottage on a hillside. But it is seen in relation to the larger scale of the surrounding hills and sky, roads, paths and trees. If it is your intention to emphasize the sense of isolation, then scale will be important and you will draw the cottage from a greater distance. If, on the other hand, you are concerned with the textural qualities of the stone of the cottage, then you will have to come much closer to the subject. In this way the

In this drawing after Seurat's *Port-En-Bessin*, or *The Outer Harbour, High Tide*, you can see how important it was that Seurat's pointillist technique rested on a carefully composed underlying structure — otherwise the elements in the image would not have related to each other. Here, the predominant horizontals establish the levels of recession into the distance and emphasize the calmness of the scene.

Left: this drawing is after Cézanne's work *The Bridge at Mennecy*, which was one of his most classic and mature paintings. **Below:** I have analyzed the main elements of the composition in the drawing on the left and reduced them to their simplest forms. What this exercise reveals is that the composition is based on verticals and horizontals which are carefully balanced.

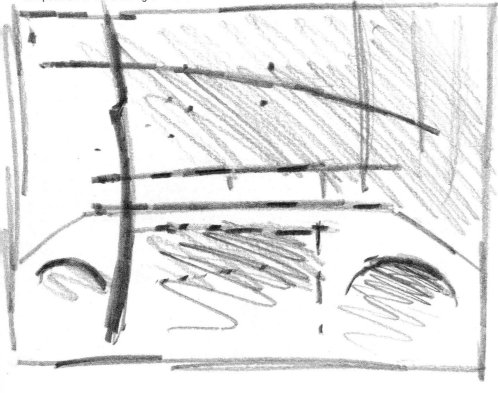

composition of a painting is determined by your intentions.

In painting seascapes, particularly, the composition is dependent on where the line of the horizon is placed. If, for instance, the main theme of the painting is an atmospheric stormy sky, then you would place the horizon low in the composition to emphasize the sky's dominance.

The division of space known as the "Golden Section" is the best known device for dividing space aesthetically. The simplest way of finding the Golden Section in any given rectangle is to take a sheet of paper of the size you are working to and fold it in half three times in succession (do this for both the length and breadth of the paper). The folds will divide the paper into eight equal parts, from which a 3:5 ratio can be determined. (Alternative ratios might be 2:3, 5:8, or 8:13.) This device works best in compositions where there are few elements, usually some insignificant vertical structure or perhaps a tree. It happens that we sometimes unconsciously place the most significant element approximately in relation to the Golden Section anyway. Intuition can play an important part in composing a painting.

Classical painters also used various pictorial devices to lead the eye towards the most critical part of their composition. Rivers and paths, or trees positioned at regular intervals, were employed to encourage the eye to travel

Above: I painted this view of the boatyard at Appledore from close quarters so that the sheds and slipway almost dominate the scene. However, the few houses indicated in the background increase the overall feeling of space.

Right: this is the same scene as above, but painted from further away, using paler colours to imply greater distance.

Below: in this painting, done with tempera on cardboard, the colour is more opaque because of the medium, but the darker sky helps the composition by counteracting the delicacy of the light tones.

The presence of minerals in the soil often produces unexpected colour relationships, as in this view of a tilled field in Tuscany. Its rich red colour, which comes from the mineral bauxite, creates a striking stripe between shades of its complementary colour, green. The single house sited at the edge of the field is almost compressed by the blocks of red and green. The solidity of the horizontal bands is relieved by the vertical pole and tree, and softened by the double curve of the forested hills in the background.

In this scene of Roussillon, in France, my eye was caught by the houses, which are the same ochre tint as the land on which they are built. (Roussillon derives from *roux*, which means reddish.) I particularly liked the effect of the varying shades of ochre, which created a pattern of differently coloured blocks receding into the distance. As in the image above, the reds contrast with the green of the trees.

toward the focal point of the painting. But the rules of composition should never be applied too strictly. To do so would be to produce drawings and paintings which are too self-conscious and stilted. In fact, the best test of a well-composed painting ought to be that we are unaware that the artist has imposed any predetermined plan on the work in question.

It is important to consider the tonal design of your composition – the way that three-dimensional objects are represented pictorially by light and dark shapes.

Landscape is never still – it is in a continuous state of movement and evolution. How can the landscape artist take account of the rhythmic aspect of nature? Cézanne complained "the contours escape me", but his use of colour patches overlaid at the contour take account of the vibrancy of nature. In the later paintings of Van Gogh, the rhythmic forces are very strong and full of energy: waves of corn, cypress and moving cloud are depicted by a thick impasto of opposing brush strokes. But, again, much depends on the essential character of the place where you have chosen to work – the rhythmic components of the landscape may be so gentle as to be barely perceptible.

In considering the composition of your painting you need to be aware of contrast, light and tone, scale, rhythm and the relationship between all these things together. But above all, your work should reveal a sense of place, it should reveal the fact that you have discovered and evaluated the things you have seen.

The artist William Gilpin said that, "Nature's alphabet consists only of four letters: wood, water, rock and ground. And yet within these four letters she forms such varied compositions, such infinite combinations, as no language with an alphabet of twenty-four can describe."

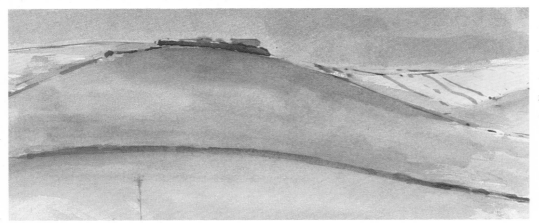

Above: in this linocut of a Cornish estuary, by Richard Vicary, the artist had to simplify the forms to their basic shapes because of the nature of the linocut process. The rich colour is produced by overprinting three separate blocks of colour. He has composed the image well, with areas of solid, dark colour counterbalanced by lighter, textured areas, and an off-centre point of interest created by the boat.

Left: the presence of chalk in a landscape has the effect of neutralizing the colour, as you can see here in the pastel hues of this image. I decided to be selective when composing this image and concentrated on the softness of the colours enhanced by the gentle undulations of the hills. Because the colours were so soft, I needed to strengthen the shapes, so drew darker outlines on the ridges.

Right: when painting this Tuscan landscape I particularly liked the contrast between the dark and light tones, and the way the different crops on the rounded hills produced a varied patterned effect. The focal point of the painting is the cluster of farm buildings and the cypress trees which, like black candles, punctuate the landscape.

Below: in this oil painting entitled *Going Home*, the direction in which the children are running is the same as the point of convergence of the three main horizontal lines — the sand, waves and background. This gives the painting movement. The sense that the children are going home at the end of the day is exaggerated by their movement into the dark left from the sunlit right.

LIGHT, MOOD AND ATMOSPHERE

In every region, no matter which country you find yourself working, there is a certain season and a certain time of day when the quality of light and the climate are most suited to reveal the intrinsic qualities of the place.

In northern Europe, every season offers the landscape painter a fresh viewpoint. In England, especially, the complete unpredictability of the weather pattern, changing as it does not just from day to day, but sometimes from hour to hour, can make life difficult for the artist who leaves his or her studio to work in the open. One of the reasons why watercolour is considered the "English" medium is that it is so evocative of this changing weather pattern.

The chalkland where I live looks best after rain in spring or autumn. Elsewhere, lakes, mountains and certain coastal regions look more atmospheric in soft summer rain. In southern Europe and in certain states in the USA, the light is more intense and contrasts are more sharply delineated. Sometimes one needs to be patient, perhaps waiting several months for exactly the right conditions of light and climate. This is only possible, of course, if your subject is not too far away.

Nature is full of contrasting shapes — the "soft" foliage of a tree seen against a brick barn for instance. There are many negative and positive elements which complement each other. In seascapes, particularly, there are often striking contrasts between a ragged coastline and the smooth glassiness of the sea.

Structure in landscape is not always immediately apparent. The shapes are generally softer. But underlying the foliage of a tree there is an intricate skeletal structure. There are a great many other structures which are concealed or half-concealed, holding the whole mass of organic matter together. It is important to be aware of this underlying structure in

Above: for this painting of Aberllefenni in Wales, the first drawing was made during a rainstorm. John Armstrong is an artist who clearly enjoys working on site, whatever the weather. He occasionally covers himself with a large sheet of polythene, making a kind of transparent protective tent, so that he can continue working in the rain. He conveys the sense of rain in this drawing with loose, quick penmarks scribbled over the mountain.
Right: in the second drawing, the artist has made colour notes of the scene in his own, abbreviated code. There is a greater amount of shading in this drawing which intensifies the darkness and the sense of impending storm.

With the aid of reference drawings and what he has been able to commit to memory, the artist distills the information of the scene he wants to paint in the form of a colour sketch. In this sketch he explores colour and compositional ideas.

The final painting was done in oil on board. The artist has resolved the question of the colours he wanted to use by restricting them to yellow and ochre hues, which contrast with the slate grey of the distant hills. The yellow is an optimistic colour and creates a feeling that sunshine is about to emerge from behind the rainclouds.

John Armstrong

Above: the influence of Turner is clearly evident in this painting. The sketches for it were made directly from observation during a hailstorm, and the marks scratched through the oil were probably made with the handle of a paintbrush.

Right: the dark cloud-shadow spreading over the valley and the cross-hatched turbulence in the sky suggest an oncoming rainstorm.

Left: acrylic has been used in washes in this image and applied like watercolour. The two tones used — blue-black and ochre — suggest the time of day and also convey the simple beauty of this still, evening scene.

Below: using media such as soft and oil pastels, mixed with paints, such as gouache, you can create a marvellous sense of swirling clouds and wind, as in this image of a Brittany landscape.

Above: in this tempera painting on gesso panel, the artist Carolyn Trant has created a convincing image of the marvellous tracery of a quince tree's bare branches. The colours are lyrical and light, sunny rather than grey, which suggests late autumn or early spring rather than winter.

Below: the sombre atmosphere of this scene of a fishing village on a dull day is captured in heavy, low-key tones. They are relieved by only a few spots of bright colour, on the houses and boats.

landscape; even the most minute forms in nature have some kind of structural support.

The geology of any region will influence the appearance of the landscape. It is your task to uncover the essential qualities and characteristics of the place you happen to be working in and to try to evoke them in your painting. In a chalkland landscape, for example, the land forms tend to be soft, and the presence of chalk in the soil neutralizes the colour, whereas in a limestone region the land forms are more irregular and punctuated by outcrops of exposed rock. The landscape artist is concerned with the appearance of things. I

Below: this painting, in oil on board, demonstrates the way that snow can link and isolate forms in an almost abstract pattern. The moon is the only visible source of light, illuminating the snow and casting an eerie cold blue haze over the scene.

might not happen to like the idea of electricity pylons being placed across the land where I live for example. Visually, however, I might like the relationship between such a man-made structure and the surrounding landscape.

We are all too often more attentive to the representation of detail than we are to the influence of light, but every landscape is made up of gradations of light and dark areas. Our awareness of light is sometimes precipitated by a sudden incident — a shaft of light piercing dense cloud illuminates a wall on a hillside, or perhaps looking into bright sunlight we see how things tend to be reduced to silhouettes.

Light waves are conditioned by the way that they react to various substances — water, cumulus cloud, stone, metal and so on. Even under direct sunlight the actual intensity of light varies considerably from one part of the landscape to another. There are various factors which affect the qualities of light — the amount of pollution and carbon dioxide in the air, for instance, the density of cloud or the quantity of dust in the atmosphere. This is further affected by the position of the sun in the sky. At sunrise and sunset the long waves of light are scattered

by dust and moisture in the atmosphere, and the sun takes on a rich red-ochre hue. This is especially beautiful when it touches the edges of clouds. At dusk or sunrise when the overall illumination is less intense the contrasts are softer. At midday, when the sun is overhead, contrasts are sharper and the light is harsher.

The mood and atmosphere of a painting is also dependent on the state of mind of the person producing it. Nothing is more self-relevatory than a drawing or painting produced from direct observation. Landscape is a personal affair; one person might like to paint in valleys, another on a high ridge of windswept hills. The work of some poets, painters and writers is often inextricably linked to a particular place which somehow reflects their mood, and which in turn feeds their imagination. To read Thomas Hardy's description of Egdon Heath, or to recite lines from *Under Milkwood* by Dylan Thomas, makes one aware of how important this sense of place is to artists and writers alike. To really absorb the atmosphere of a place you need to get to know it well. I find I need to visit an area four or five times before I can uncover the spirit of the place.

WORKING ON LOCATION

The landscape artist must necessarily find a way to cope with the problems caused by working out of doors in an intemperate climate. Even Turner had difficulties. ''The rains came on early so I could not cross the Alps; twice I tried, was set back with a wet jacket and worn-out boots.''

I usually find that when I plan a drawing trip abroad, I have visions of myself working in a sun-filled valley, but more often than not it turns out to be the wettest or coldest spring or summer for forty years! I can remember trying to draw in the Rhône Valley while the "Mistral" wind was cutting through me and, more recently, trying to find a way of working in watercolour during four weeks of incessant rain in Switzerland.

While the choice of materials for working outside is very much a personal one, there are a few commonsense suggestions which might prove helpful. First, bear in mind that in order to find the right viewpoint, it may be necessary to climb to different levels or to walk considerable distances. For this reason your equipment should not be too cumbersome. I usually take a lightweight shoulder bag containing pans of watercolour, pencils and brushes, a waterpot and a plastic bottle of water, and a rag or papertowels. Instead of a sketchbook, I take a variety of paper (Arches, Fabriano, Saunders) sandwiched between two sheets of millboard, or thick cardboard, held together with fold-back clips. My only luxury item is a lightweight folding chair which folds up like a walking stick.

Nobody takes much notice of a man reading a newspaper on a park bench, but most people are curious to see what an artist is up to. In my experience I have found people to be friendly and considerate in not disturbing me when I'm drawing. Children enjoy the novelty of seeing an

Above: when planning to paint outdoors, make sure that you have just what you will need, and no more. Try to keep everything lightweight so that you don't find it difficult to carry.
Left: make sure that you have a comfortable folding stool or chair, and a drawing board or a piece of hardboard (masonite) on which to support your work.

artist at work but usually become bored by the slow progress of the work and soon drift off. Whenever possible I try to make myself as inconspicuous as possible, positioning my chair in such a way that it is difficult for anyone to approach from behind. Since all your concentration will be required for your painting it is as well to be as comfortable as possible and to have everything you need.

Having found the right viewpoint and with everything ready to start, try just sitting back and surveying the scene before you for ten minutes or so. Then, when you are ready to start drawing, begin right away to secure those aspects of the scene which determine your intentions. Perhaps you first need to establish the contour of a hill or the horizon line dividing sea and sky. As you slowly register the main parts of your drawing, you will notice how everything begins to relate to each other on the surface of the paper. Colour and tone will start to unify the composition. When all your intentions have been realized, then the painting is finished. The difficulty lies in recognizing when you have reached that point!

Right: I find that a few selected pastels for making an underdrawing or colour notes, and two boxes of chosen watercolours with lids that I can mix the colours in, are sufficient when I work outdoors. I usually also carry a small range of pencils and brushes to give me some variety.
Below: working in the open air in England is quite different from working in a hot country, and I am full of admiration for Ian Potts, who worked in Egypt. On his trip down the Nile he suffered physically from the discomfort of mud huts and digestive disorders. But he was still exhilarated by the colours he saw, the contrasts between the desert and the delta, and the sights on the Nile itself. He filled several sketchbooks which made perfect reference material to be worked up later. This painting of the Nile, near Aswan, was worked up from several sketches done on site.

WHITE CLIFFS

The white chalk cliffs known as the "Seven Sisters", happen to be only minutes from where I live. From Seaford Head the cliffs undulate for about a mile towards the direction of Beachy Head. Like the cliffs at Dover, they are often used as a kind of romantic symbol of an England that has stood defiant against invading armies throughout the centuries.

One of the problems of drawing or painting a popular scene is that you have probably seen the same images filtered through many different sources — postcards, posters, travel guides and even on teacloths. Then there are countless renderings by local art clubs and photographic societies. You have to put all of this aside in order to see the subject anew.

This scene is painted so often with bright, gay colours that actually bear little reference to the site itself. What struck me about the colours of the sky, land and sea was that they were all neutral because of the presence of the chalk. Even the sea was opaque because of the chalk washed into it. The colours are therefore all closely related — grey ochres, grey greens, etc.

There were a number of considerations I had to bear in mind. Compositionally, I felt I wanted to emphasize the essentially horizontal aspect of the cliffs. Then there were contrasts between the chalky headlands and the sea and sky. I felt, too, that the tenuous structure of the cliffs was important. I decided that in the first instance I would draw in pencil, perhaps making a few colour notes, before beginning to work on canvas.

Walking from the top of Seaford Head towards the coastguard cottages on the lower slopes, there are endless compositional possibilities and I moved around a great deal before settling for a particular view. It is the kind of place where one could quite easily produce a series of drawings of different viewpoints without being repetitive in any way.

This drawing of the white cliffs was done on site with a soft pencil, on canvas. I chose to draw it on a grid, because I felt that this would help to sort out the compositional relationship of the elements, such as the proportions of the houses to the cliffs, the land to the sea and the sea to the sky. I then added colour notes, to refresh my memory when I painted the work in my studio.

Working on the same canvas, I applied oil paint thinned with turpentine, with a hog's hair, no. 6, chisel-edged brush. At this stage I was concerned with getting rid of the white canvas and putting colour on as quickly as possible.

I simply wanted to sort out the basic tones — the tonal relationships could be worked out later. The main framework of the painting is established in blues and greens. The tone of the sky is wrong — it's too bright — but I knew that I could amend it later. I painted part of the structure with a fine brush and dilute dark colour to restate the drawing. The subsequent overpainting cancels out part of the drawing and leaves some of it exposed, creating a lost-and-found effect. Sometimes, if the structure gets lost in the process of painting, it needs to be restated again in this way.

Above: I used this study of the farthest cliff in the main sequence as a reference for the painting. It was done at close quarters, at an earlier stage, and I was concentrating on the crumbling coastguard cottages and the eroding coastline — it is disappearing at a rate of six metres (about eighteen feet) a year. This is a watercolour and pencil sketch, done on Ingres d'Arches laid paper.

Below: I also used this charcoal and pastel study of the cliffs from a different viewpoint as a reference. I was interested in their shapes, looking at them head on rather than along them.

In the final stages I added a grey-green tone over the sky when it was almost dry, and then tried to scrub it off with a dry rag, so that patches of blue could be seen just coming through. I also added opaque colour tentatively over the ridges of the cliffs, to highlight their contours. The tone of the sea has been made darker to emphasize the whiteness of the chalk. At this point I painted in the coastguard cottages. I resisted the temptation to overpaint and pick out individual details, the blades of grass, etc., to keep the painting at the same level of development. I felt that to add more detail would be superfluous and wanted to try and keep its spontaneity.

All the colours were mixed with flake white, which neutralizes the tones and exaggerates the chalky characteristics of the scene.

SWISS LAKES

The impact that the Swiss lakes makes comes mostly from their atmosphere — one can well appreciate why Turner felt so drawn to Switzerland. When I was asked to produce a series of some 35 drawings and paintings to commemorate the 150th anniversary of the Lake of Lucerne Steamboat Company, I was given a free pass to travel at will on the boats, which enabled me to explore various locations along the lake. Though I was at times irritated by almost incessant rain, I somehow came to terms with the weather, and realized that the mountains and lakes are actually more interesting in such conditions. There were a number of practical problems, such as needing to know where the light would fall at different times of day. I found that mountains on one side of the lake did not get much light before mid-afternoon, for instance. The best views were from the boats, and indeed Turner, sailing on the same lake, made numerous pencil sketches from steamboats.

Using a timetable I was able to work out when I could expect a steamboat to appear at a certain point on the lake. This meant that I had to draw the background landscape an hour or so before the boat arrived. When the boat did appear, I had to draw it quickly, since even paddle boats move quite rapidly through the water. When the weather was really bad, I made drawings below deck on the boats, including studies of children watching the huge pistons of the engine. On fine days I made more detailed studies of the boats and lakeside architecture.

This watercolour of the steamboat approaching Bauen was painted on Arches paper with a broad brush. First, I tentatively established the contours of the mountains with a pencil line, and then laid broad washes of colour. I then painted the background mountains and much of the foreground, working for about three hours before the steamboat arrived in the position I wanted. I had only a few seconds to incorporate it into the painting.

I took a mountain railway halfway up the Righi mountain to paint the lake from a higher level. It is sometimes difficult to decide just how much to leave out from a view. I could, for instance, have dealt more with the trees and foliage in the foreground, but this might have detracted too much from the other elements in the composition. I laid two or three washes here, in pale grey, yellow grey and a darker grey to suggest the misty atmosphere.

Left: this view of the steamboat approaching Flüelen is from the famous Axenstrasse. Although I produced the painting during a rainstorm, I was able to work under the protection of the arches of the road tunnel. It was freezing cold and there was fresh snow on the mountains — and this was only August. I worked part of the image wet-on-wet, allowing the colours to merge, to portray the rain and mist on the mountains.

Right: this painting was done in an apple orchard by the lakeside, towards the end of a rare, fine afternoon. The tones were delicate but clear in the pellucid haze. I liked their simplicity and so decided to put in very little detail.

Below: this painting was produced in the studio from two separate reference drawings. I had made a pencil drawing of the steamboat berthed in Lucerne and at another time painted the background landscape, looking across the lake from Vitznau. I wanted to make the white of the boat stand out from the background, and so made the mountains particularly dark. I also exaggerated the scale tremendously, to make the lake seem larger and the mountains farther away.

Top left: I consider this painting to be unfinished. I had worked for about two-and-a-half hours, when heavy squalls of driving rain made working in watercolour impossible. Nevertheless, it does express something of the atmosphere of the place. I strengthened the contours on the left by drawing them with a brush, and balanced their delicacy by darkening the shadow on the mountain and forest on the right.

Left: this pencil and watercolour was done in a cave on the lakeside to get the right viewpoint. The areas on the edge are painted wet-on-wet to depict the softness of the rain and mist. I inserted the steamboat in the few seconds that it remained stationary. In this kind of painting there is no time for second thoughts — you have to make a bold statement, which either works or doesn't.

Below: I sat on a raft floating on the lake to produce this painting of the steamboat berthed in Lucerne. The main difficulty was that every time a boat went by, it rocked the raft uncontrollably. Eventually, I abandoned the work, because I felt that it was an unsatisfactory composition. I like bits of it, but as a whole it doesn't work — the viewpoint is not right, everything is at the same level.

Right: having concentrated on the steamboats and the lakes for some time, I needed to draw people for a change. This was one of a number of pencil drawings I made below decks of children gathered excitedly around the boat's guard rails to watch its huge pistons driving the paddles.

VENICE

Venice is a fascinating city — inspiring yet elusive. So many artists have tried to distill and uncover her essential charm, yet rarely do their ideas coincide. Nothing could be more different for instance, than the almost photographic rendering of detail by Canaletto, and the misty vagueness and near abstraction of Turner.

Which of the hundreds of faces that Venice presents can an artist hope to show? It is both a land- and sea-scape flanked by exquisite decaying architecture that reflects its position at the trade crossroads between East and West.

Nothing can prepare one for the visual shock of seeing Venice for the first time, and I have some sympathy for the American who was reported to have sent a cable home saying, "All streets flooded, please advise"!

The main problem for the artist is one of

access; so many beautiful vistas beckon, but it can be frustrating and difficult to find a place with enough space to work. I did the painting of S. Maria della Salute from an awkward position, sitting on a wall. I had to rest frequently because of cramp in one leg and a constant flow of tourists disembarking from the *vaporetti*. Additionally, at midday in August the sun pounded mercilessly on my white watercolour paper (some artists use a toned paper for this reason). I used colour very sparingly because I wanted to retain the feeling for light.

Above: Venice provides the artist with a unique opportunity to produce paintings which are both landscapes and seascapes. This painting of the San Giorgio Maggiore from the Zattere was done on Fabriano 100% cotton paper. It is a painting from a painting, and I prefer the original because the colours were better — here they are too stark. In Italian skies there always appear to be a touch of red, which is why I have added rose madder to the blue of the sky here.

Left: I produced this large painting in watercolour in the studio, working from the reference drawing. Certain problems arise when you change the scale from a drawing to a painting. More attention must be given to architectural detail, for instance, but you must be careful to retain the sense of spontaneity of the original sketch.

Above: whenever I work in Venice, I become very conscious of the fact that to truly know a place you must draw it first. I produced this drawing *in situ* of the Santa Maria della Salute at midday. The colour was deliberately used sparingly because, by leaving undrawn areas white, it helped to convey the intensity of the light. It is not always necessary to fill the entire surface.

ATHENS

Ian Potts

The Acropolis stood almost intact until the arrival of a Venetian mortar shell in 1613, which shattered the roof and central shrines of the Parthenon. The remains are nevertheless awesome especially when silhouetted against the sky.

Ian Potts walked each day from the British School in Athens to the Acropolis, during a four-week study visit. Prevented by droves of tourists from reaching the level of involvement that the subject demanded, he developed a series of wash drawings spanning the brief

hours of early morning when, apart from the guards, he was almost the only inhabitant. In his choice of subject, monochromatic colour and composition, these paintings recall the classical work of Claude.

Above: working almost entirely in a blue-black wash, the artist has managed to convey a great deal about the atmosphere of this ruin on a hill above Athens. The early morning light illuminates the stone, producing a heightened sense of drama against a dark sky. The white of the raw paper contrasts starkly with the painted areas. The lines of cypresses echo the lines of the columns, and the foreground curve emphasizes the curve of the hill.

Right: this is a lucid brush drawing of the Acropolis, with no preliminary pencil drawing. All the work in this series is monochromatic because the artist felt that this was the best way of dealing with this classical subject, and that colour would simply be an intrusion.

Left: again, the sharp contrast between reflected light from the stone and the intensity of the sky creates a theatrical sense of drama, as if the building were part of a stage set.

Above and right: in these drawings of the Acropolis seen in the early morning, the artist has used ink rather than paints, applied with a broad brush on absorbent paper. The contrast of tones is reversed compared with the other drawings in the series: the Acropolis is seen as a colossal silhouette against the lighter tones of the sky. The dimensions of the paintings emphasize the feeling of space and grandeur, and the long, horizontal proportions are closely related to Claude's paintings.

EGYPT

Ian Potts

In 1985 Ian Potts made a solo journey down the Nile. He found himself continually excited by what he saw, and by colours he had not experienced before. In spite of the obvious discomfort of sleeping in mud huts, and suffering digestive disorders, he was fascinated by Luxor, Aswan, the contrast between lush delta and harsh desert, the Nile and its cataracts. He produced a portfolio of sketchbooks which were aimed at supporting subsequent work. In that sense, they were "private" and not intended as final work. Yet he felt that the sketches are important in their directness. He became absorbed by the deepest blues of the Nile, contrasting with its small boats and shimmering sails against the desert background, or the unbelievable colours around the setting sun. He found that a bicycle was the best form of transport, and with an ample supply of water and his painting materials he travelled to the Valley of the Kings and the cataracts of the Nile. In every direction he found subjects worthy of visual commentary.

Above: the artist was absorbed by the deep blue of the sky, which provides a rich background for the fragments of masonry. The simple blocks of colour are held together loosely by a drawn brush line and there is very little blending. What impressed him most was the intensity of colour.

Below: this painting was produced towards dusk, when the ruins were silhouetted against a sky of intense gradations of colour. The artist laid the gradated wash first, merging cold blue and warm pink-red very subtly. He then applied more formal brushwork in the structure of the columns, laid over the washes. The brushwork is particularly delicate on the palms.

The window acts as a kind of frame here, trapping the brilliant colour of the Nile and the shimmering sails of boats against the desert background. It is painted predominantly with shades of blue, which contrast with the warm sand colours of the desert. Some of the colour seems to have been sponged. This is a good example of a watercolour painted with brush and colour and nothing else — it is a watercolour in the purest sense.

TUSCANY

Tuscany represents the classic Virgilian ideal — vines, cypresses and olive trees set among rustic and noble architecture in gentle undulating hills. No wonder, then, that it has attracted so many artists and writers over the centuries. The intensity of light is such that it is often best to work in early morning, or late afternoon. Hill towns such as San Gimignano, Monteriggioni and Volterra, have a spectacular setting. There are so many potential subjects that it is often difficult to know where to start. Tuscany is exceptionally beautiful, but . . . what goes on there? Apart from painting landscapes which are a delight to behold there are other subjects worth seeking out. The stone quarries at Carrara, for instance, provide a great deal of visual interest with the huge slabs of marble catching the light. Street markets too are full of animated colour.

The series of paintings here were painted from a hotel window which overlooked the countryside. Waking early, I saw the distant cypress-covered hills shrouded in mist. Then, as it became warmer, the mist began to rise slowly until everything was sharply defined. I used white gouache with watercolour on a toned paper in order to strike a balance between the opaque and translucent qualities of the scene, and to suggest forms half-concealed, half-revealed by mist. The colours were closely related in tone.

Top left: this was the first study of the series, done on the balcony of my hotel at 6.30a.m. I was unsure how to handle the veils of early morning mist in terms of watercolour, but using a toned paper helped considerably. The colour was monochromatic at this stage because of the still dull light, restricted to grey, grey-green, and blue-black.

Above: half an hour later, the dark silhouette of cypresses on the brow of the hill became visible and the mist began to rise from the ground, but the colours were still fairly monochromatic.

Left: this painting was done at 7.30a.m. I took a lot of risks with it, working wet-on-wet, pushing the image around and hoping that nothing would be lost as the paint dried. I mixed opaque white with watercolour to create the semi-opaque layers of mist.

Above: in this painting of boilers during demolition, there are just two or three washes; the texture is expressed with loosely drawn brushwork. The granular quality of the boiler structure is achieved by mixing a lot of pigment in the water so that when it dries it has a gritty appearance which suggests rusting metal.

Left: the colour in this wharfside painting is almost monochromatic, save for the red of the telephone box and the blue noticeboards. The light and dark tones are expressed purely with washes. These flat washes contrast with the very intricate detail of the individual bricks and lettering, painted with a fine brush. The white of the brickwork is the white of the paper — each brick has been painstakingly painted in.

Above: some industrial architecture blends naturally with the landscape and provides visual interest in an otherwise dull scene. I drew these cement works in pencil from a high vantage point and then applied washes loosely with a no. 3 brush. By mixing white gouache with the watercolour I produced an opaque quality in the chalk and the smoke in the sky. Some areas were deliberately left undeveloped.

Above: coal-fired power stations seem to possess the same kind of monumentality as medieval cathedrals; the strong composition of this image carries this across. Andrew Laws worked on site while this station was being demolished and then finished the painting back in the studio, adding the detail. He uses colour to effect in the red barrier, the corrugated iron, and the noticeboard. He lays washes meticulously and doesn't allow anything to bleed.

Below: the power station breaking into the sky makes a single powerful element. This is a key picture in the series because it shows the station in its totality whereas the other paintings depict and develop aspects of it.

Left: this painting of the power station during demolition is not as tightly controlled as the others, which makes it, I think, more effective. A few softer tones have been allowed to creep in and there are some wet-on-wet tones in the sky. In many of his industrial landscapes Andrew Laws uses a single figure to give a sense of scale and add a human element.

BUILDINGS IN LANDSCAPE

Ruskin believed that the authenticity of landscape painting depended on some kind of reference to man. Architecture provides this reference as well as creating a point of interest in the landscape. Churches, agricultural buildings, stone cottages and castles are a means of punctuating what might otherwise be a featureless scene. The contrasts of light and shade are more critical when dealing with architecture, and sources of light need to be clearly defined. The precise relationship of the building to the surrounding landscape needs to be thought about carefully: a building set on a ridge might look more dramatic from a distance, but may be less interesting as you come closer to it; conversely, the textural qualities of a stone barn must be seen at close range. Much depends on what you hope to extract from a particular place. At one time it was easy to distinguish one region from another, by the use of local stone and timber employed for buildings.

Below: what interested me most in this scene of the Basilica of St Francis at Assisi was the relationship between the arches and the trees. Although it is the kind of work where you need to state only some architectural detail and the rest barely at all, the main workload in this drawing was the arches — there are some 50 of them — and the image took about four to five hours to complete in situ.

Above: in this image of the shopfronts at Dieppe the main structure was drawn in pencil and the balcony and shopfronts were drawn with a brush. The sea mists and rain have weathered the colours on the buildings into interesting tones. Also, as it was a grey day, the colours were tonally quite dark.

Above: in this pencil and watercolour painting of Santa Croce in Florence, the various architectural elements are linked by the tone of the distant hills and the natural forms of the trees and fields. The architectural detail of the church is the main point of interest, and I liked the relationship between the church and the tower on the right in the foreground. The pencil helps to define the architectural structure.

Left: in this pastel, the main shapes are defined in flat tones of chalk. The artist then used black, red and grey crayon to bring the linear elements together and strengthen the main structure of the dome and church. She has applied white over the colours to create a sense of haze. It is a rapidly drawn work with strong gestural strokes and a sense of urgency.

Below: this country church was painted in watercolours in a fine rain which further diluted the paint as it was being applied to the paper. The pencil sketch is still apparent under the washes, which were laid wet-on-wet to merge the colours.

Above: the long proportions of this barn parallel the horizontal aspect of the landscape. The underpainting of the grass is overlaid with wash and then worked over later. Pattern is created with stippling and brushwork. Where natural materials from the area are used in buildings, they become part of the landscape, as with this barn. But where man-made or "imported" materials are used, the buildings become conspicuous.

LOUDS, SKY AND THE SEA

Wendy Murphy

It is ... w many artists fail to recognize tha... e sky is an integral part of a landscape or seascape composition. John Constable, in a letter to the Rev. John Fisher, says, "the landscape painter who does not make his skies a very material part of his composition neglects to avail himself of one of his greatest aids." The sky is the source of light in landscape. The quality of light can greatly influence the mood or heighten the drama of a painting. Even a clear cloudless sky changes

Right: there are times when tones merge in such a way that it becomes difficult to discern where the horizon meets the sky, particularly where the predominantly dark hue of the sea influences the tone of the sky. Here, the artist is concerned more with the atmosphere created by these tones than with the sea itself. She is working in oil on coloured paper. Working on paper means that you do not have to worry about the cost of the material and may make you more inclined to experiment with colours and techniques.

Left: where you place the horizon is important in giving emphasis to the sky. The beach in this painting occupies three-quarters of the total area of the painting, so that the sea appears to be confined to a fine band of colour trapped between shore and sky. The extent of the sand in the foreground is relieved by the whites of the waves.

Above: the brush strokes in this tranquil picture of a calm sea at sunset are very attractive; their broad quality prevents the image from becoming too picturesque and clichéd.

Above right: the choppiness of this sea and the bands of rain striking the waves like an axe are achieved with diagonal strokes of the brush. The artist is using the brush dry, with very little paint on it to create the choppy texture.

Below: the sea is very difficult to paint without making it look static or too opaque. Here the artist has used short brushstrokes of colour on the ridges of the waves to give a sense of choppy movement which is very convincing. The way oil can be scumbled and impastoed suits the sea because it can imply the movement of water.

Sophie Mason

from dawn to dusk and it will never be even in tone. From the skyline upwards there may be many hues and soft gradations of colour with hints of rose madder or red-blue, depending on the intensity of the light.

Constable often made the sky a key note in his painting; his native East Anglia is low-lying so that the horizon line is often placed quite low in his compositions.

Clouds provide a point of interest — they lend a sense of recession and depth. It is useful to make separate studies of clouds as an exercise in understanding how the forms vary. Clouds are not always white — they often have a soft underbelly of tone, and again this can add to the drama of a landscape view.

Try not to think of the sky as a separate shape tacked onto the horizon. Turner, for instance, managed to convey veils of atmosphere in his paintings, particularly in his studies of Venice where there is no separation between sea and sky.

Above: pastel and gouache are handled vigorously in this drawing to render the shifting cloud patterns. All the movement is in the sky, which takes up three-quarters of the image. Its dynamic quality is enhanced by the static nature of the landscape and the way the artist has picked out shapes randomly with white chalk.

Above: in this drawing of Hastings Pier, highlighted against dramatic stormclouds, the artist has blended the tones more, pushing the colour about with her fingertips. She has used pastel, chalk and charcoal, smudging the charcoal to blend the colours and pick out the contours in the drawing. The way the light hits the side of the pier is very attractive.

Right: the pastel in this sky is almost calligraphic in its strokes. They express well the squalls of raincloud with intermittent patches of sunlight breaking through and illuminating the acid green fields.

Left: this pastel and gouache landscape bathed in sunlight under a clear sky is very different in character to the painting above. It has been captured very quickly, using the pastel strokes to give it a sense of direction: on the ground they are horizontal and on the sky they are vertical.

TREES

Trees are perhaps the most conspicuous vertical elements that we see in a landscape view. But it would be wrong to think of trees simply as a useful aid — every tree has its own shape and character. The immense variety of specimens lends a special character to every region. The apple tree of Normandy for instance, is very different in form and texture to the candle-like cypress of southern Europe.

It is common for most artists to experience difficulty with finding the right way to express the foliage of a tree. Try to draw the main and secondary shapes first; leaves can be indicated later. The shape of a tree is described by its branches and the overall shape of the foliage. Even when drawing trees in the foreground of your composition you should be selective — don't try to draw every leaf. Too much attention to such detail will make your painting look flat. Try to draw the trunk and branches with the same kind of searching sensitivity you would employ for a figure drawing. Do not draw trees according to your own preconceived ideas of what they should look like — instead try to discover the particular qualities that makes one tree different from another.

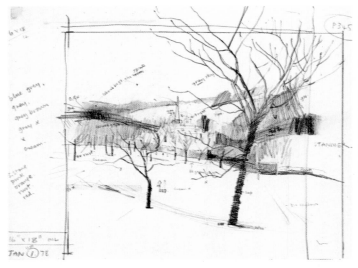

Above: this tree study by John Armstrong is a lively drawing produced with a soft pencil on cartridge (drawing paper). There is a sense that the artist is exploring the direction of the branches, their pattern and shape.

Above right: this is a reference drawing for the painting opposite. Even though it is spare in its information the main composition is sorted out and the artist has recorded the branch shapes in detail.

Below: there is a great deal of intricate detail in this deceptively simple landscape, which conveys the artist's love of the landscape. She takes an area of the countryside and studies it intensively, as if to make it her own. The colour relationships are delightful, contrasting the purple of the sky with the green trees and grass. It is done in tempera on gesso panel.

Carolyn Trant's studies of nature stem from intensive observation of the places she knows best. Over long periods of time, she follows the gradual changes through different seasons and under different conditions of light. This painting of willows reflects her tremendous powers of observation, seeing how every tree and its branches overlay and work together; there is no invention here but painstaking application. This painting was done in tempera on a gesso panel.

Snow changes the appearance of things quite dramatically — it has a wonderful unifying effect and produces sharp contrasts of tone. The skeletal structure of winter trees become even more conspicuous and the sky darker in tone than the snow-covered landscape. This landscape was painted in oil on board.

RIVERS

Anthony Colbert

Rivers are one of the main rhythmic elements in landscape. Additionally, they offer the repetition of landscape forms in reflection. Shapes reflected in water are softened tonally — darks appear lighter and lights darker. Water has a surface which is difficult to represent. Monet in his studies of water lilies managed to convey both surface qualities and a sense of depth. The tones of water are deceptive and need to be constantly checked against the river bank, trees and surrounding forms.

Above right: Anthony Colbert has combined flat areas of colour, using the acrylic like a watercolour wash, giving emphasis to the sky and conveying stillness with the reflections in the smooth water.

Left: in this marshland scene, with the sun just disappearing behind cloud, the artist has created a marvellous relationship between cool and warm tones. The detail on the horizon is expressed with a single tone of grey which is absolutely delicious.

Above: in this painting, the acrylic paint has been used more thickly. It is a good example of a mirror image, which you get only with still water. Again, the artist has achieved a wonderful balance between the warm and cool tones.

Right: there is a lovely relationship in this painting between sky and water, divided only by a very narrow strip of detail on the horizon. The way the artist has treated the light on the surface of the water gives it a good sense of depth. To contrast with the overall smoothness, he has used light, deft brushwork to indicate the grass in the foreground, and has picked out detail randomly with a fine brush.

BEACH SCENES

Ken Howard ARA

This series of beach scenes was produced in Cornwall where painters have long recognized the special quality of light. Light is essentially Ken Howard's main concern; he is particularly interested in working *contre jour* – against the light. He expresses light through tone rather than colour, working with closely related earth colours and reserving primary colours to make the occasional jarring note in his compositions.

Working directly from the subject in oil, watercolour and mixed media, these studies possess a freshness and sense of spontaneity which cannot be achieved when working from reference away from the subject.

Ken Howard describes his painting as being celebratory in the sense that he finds so many subjects which are visually beautiful and stimulating that he feels the need to say something about them. He believes that each painter should recognize where his or her vision lies, and then concentrate on developing that.

Above: this oil on canvas, of an August evening, is a good example of a painting produced against the light, or *contre jour*. The tone of the sky suggests the warmth of a summer evening. The shadows are extended and link the various groups of people on the beach. The light touches the edge of forms and illuminates the windbreaks.

Above: the loose handling of the paint suggests an attempt to capture moving figures in situ and has the feeling of having been done very rapidly. The balance and position of the boat sails contribute to the success of the composition. The effect of light on water is beautifully expressed; everything in the painting counts and there is no unnecessary detail.

Right: by choosing this subject matter the artist can contrast bright primary colours with natural earth colours. The colours of boat sails and windbreaks are a foil to the more muted tones of land and sea. Additionally, they serve to define space in the composition. Some figures are expressed in a fraction of a second as a single statement of the brush, but they are convincingly stated in a way that can come only from working directly from observation.

Left: here, windbreaks are used both as a link between the figures and the beach, and to provide a visual connection between the foreground, middle distance and the horizon, rather like a zigzag. The brilliance of light in that part of the Cornish peninsula is suggested in the high key of the colours. The artist laid the ground on his canvas to establish the tone of the beach and sea, and then set the people down very quickly because they were moving all the time.

Above: this diminutive sketch has the same kind of humour that Bonnard sometimes allowed into his paintings. It was done in pencil, gouache and watercolour. The windbreak was painted in translucent washes which reveal shadows, created by the underlying pencil. The dog is loosely expressed in wash. White flecks of gouache body colour have been applied to suggest light catching waves on water.

Below: the most striking element of this painting is the blue and yellow light shining through the windbreak, which produces a kind of stained-glass effect. A wash was laid over the whole paper, with the exception of the windbreak, and then splashes of colour were laid over the sand afterwards – the pebbles have been expressed with a flick of the brush. Ken Howard tends to express standing figures with one tone. He doesn't worry about their contours, and just paints them direct. Probably, the last touch

Right: this small painting displays exquisite visual judgement on the part of the artist, both in the disposition of the related elements and in the balance of tone and colour. The contrast between the pink of the windbreak and the blue-grey-green is lovely.

MOUNTING AND FRAMING

A drawing or painting will be enhanced if it is thoughtfully framed and complementary materials are used. An oil painting, if varnished, is better left unglazed to avoid bad light reflection.

Artists are not always the best judges of how their work should be mounted/matted and framed. If we feel too close to a piece of work that we have just produced, for instance, the detached view of a friend or a professional framer can be helpful. It is important to remember that the main purpose of mounting/matting and framing is to provide your work with a border that will offset it against a wall – a discreetly formal frame might do this much better than an over-ornate gilded frame, which could detract from the painting itelf. The mounting/matting and presentation of paintings and drawings is a craft in its own right. A well-proportioned mount/mat and frame can enhance a painting as well as isolating it from its immediate surroundings.

Watercolours, gouaches, pastels and drawings require window mounts/mats with generous borders. Acid-free or museum-quality boards are less prone to discoloration. You should also use an acid-free tape to secure the paper to the mount/mat. Generally, a white or cream mount/mat is most suitable for drawings. Neutral tints are best for watercolours and pastels, though in some instances a richly coloured mount/mat might be more appropriate. If you are able to borrow framers' samples, you can test the colour against the painting before buying the board. Likewise with sample frames, the corners can be placed on the painting in turn until the most suitable moulding is found. Window mounts/mats also serve the more practical purpose of keeping the painting or drawing away from contact with the glass. The window shape cut from the card should be set above centre so that the bottom margin is proportionally larger than the remaining sides. If you decide to cut your own mounts/mats, there are now a variety of different mat-cutters available. Most have an adjustable blade so that the cut is bevelled. You will also need a good stainless steel straightedge. Stainless steel or plain wooden mouldings are sometimes best for drawings.

Watercolours and pastels can be enhanced by a narrow half-round gilt or silver frame. Oil paintings might benefit from wider mouldings with a linen inset in contact with the canvas.

Most framers usually have a stock of slightly soiled or damaged frames which can be bought inexpensively and made good. Alternatively, old frames can sometimes be bought in furniture sales.

Corner samples of mounts/mats and frames are useful for testing colours and types of moulding against the painting. The mount/mat can relate to colours used in the painting or be completely neutral. Be careful when you choose mounts/mats and frames, because if they are overly decorative they will only detract from the painting itself.

GLOSSARY

Academic
This term refers to a style of painting or drawing which follows traditional methods without further development or experiment.

Acrylic
A paint made from pigment suspended in synthetic resin. It has only been fully developed in recent years; it has great permanence, and is quick-drying and colourfast.

Alla Prima
Painting directly onto a support in a single session, without a preliminary underpainting or drawing.

Atmosphere
Relates to the suggested recession in a painting, achieved with changes in tone and colour between the foreground and background.

Body Colour
Essentially, white gouache. It can also refer to watercolour paint mixed with white gouache to make it opaque.

Blending
Merging colours together, with a brush, torchon or fingertip, so that no sharp divisions of colour are visible.

Classical
A term which refers to drawings and paintings that strive towards established ideals of perfection.

Cold (of colour)
All colours can be related to sensations of warmth or cold. Warm colours tend toward yellows, cold toward blues.

Complementary colours
A colour is complementary to the colour with which it contrasts most strongly, such as red and green. Complementary colours are found opposite each other on the colour wheel.

Composition
The satisfactory arrangement of all the related elements in a painting.

Cross-hatching
Layers of crisscrossed parallel lines, usually done with a pen or pencil, and used as a means of shading.

Drawing-in
The initial statement of the drawing on the painting surface.

Dry-brush
A technique in which excess water or thinner is squeezed out of the brush. This leaves a residue of dry pigment, which is then applied to a surface, and creates a textured, granular quality.

Figurative
A term which reflects the artist's intention of representing natural forms.

Fixative
A thin transparent varnish which is sprayed onto the surface of a drawing to make it stable, i.e. to stop the pigment from coming off the support or smudging.

Form
A term which refers to the three-dimensional appearance of a shape.

Fugitive
Used to describe colours that are liable to fade in the course of time.

Glaze
Transparent layers of colour laid over another base colour.

Ground
The ground coat of paint which makes a surface suitable for painting on. Can also be the first colour laid on the surface as a preliminary tone.

Graphite
A particular type of pencil in which the lead is made from carbon and clay.

Half-tone
A tone mid-way between black and white, or the strength between the darkest and lightest tone.

Hatching
Shading in a drawing, represented by parallel lines. Cross-hatching is done with crossed lines.

Hue
The colour, rather than the tone, of a pigment or object.

Impasto
A heavy paste-like application of paint which produces a textured effect.

Local colour
The actual colour of an object, such as the red of an apple, rather than a colour which is modified by light or shadow.

Medium
The medium is (a) the type of material used to produce a drawing or painting e.g. charcoal, pastel, gouache, oil, etc, or (b) a substance blended with paint to thicken, thin or dry the paint.

Modelling
Expressing the volume and solidity of an object with light and shade.

Monochrome
Refers to a painting done in a single colour or in tones of black and white.

Muted
Refers to colours when their full colour value is suppressed.

Opaque
Describes the density of paint. Not transparent.

Palette
This can be (a) the surface on which the colours are mixed, or (b) a particular range of colours selected individually by the artist.

Perspective
A means of recreating objects so that they look three-dimensional, or appear to have depth, on a two-dimensional surface. Linear perspective makes use of parallel lines which converge on a vanishing point. Aerial perspective suggests distance by the use of tones.

Priming
A treatment applied to canvas or board which makes the surface non-absorbent.

Scumbling
A technique whereby an opaque colour is dragged roughly across another, covering it partially.

Support
The surface on which a painting or drawing is made (canvas, wood, paper, etc.).

Tone
The light and dark value of a colour; for example, pale blue is the same tone as pale ochre but both are lighter in tone than dark brown.

Underpainting
The first laying-in of basic colours in thin transparent paint.

Wash
Diluted colour applied to paper in a way which allows it to spread evenly in a thin transparent film.

Watercolour
A paint made from colour pigment bound in gum and glycerine; it is soluble in water.

Wet-on-wet
A watercolour technique which involves adding colour on an already wet colour previously laid on the paper.

INDEX

Page numbers in *italics* refer to the illustrations and captions

A
acid-free boards, 106
acrylics, *44*, 45
architecture, 90, *90-3*
Armstrong, John, *58-9, 98*
art pencils, 19
artists' colours, watercolours, 34
Athens (Ian Potts), 80, *80-1*
atmosphere, 58, 62

B
ball-point pens, 25
bamboo pens, 25, *25*
beach scenes, 102, *102-5*
boards, mounting, 106
body colour, *see* gouache
Bonnard, Pierre, 28, *103*
brights, brushes, 32
Brueghel, Pieter, 10
brushes, 32-3, *32-3*
buildings, 90, *90-3*

C
camera obscura, 10
Canaletto, 10, 78
canvases, 43
cardboard supports, 43
Cézanne, Paul, 7, *11*, 13, 36, 39, 44, *53*, 55
chalk pastels, 22, 23, *23*
charcoal, 18, 20, *20-1*
charcoal pencils, 20
Chevreul, Michel Eugène, 13
Chinese ink, 25
Claude Lorraine, 9, 13, 80, 81
cleaning brushes, 33
cliffs, 66, *66-71*
clouds, 94-6, *94-7*
Colbert, Anthony, *Rivers, 100-1*
Coldstream, Sir William, *12*
coloured inks, 25, *25*
colours, 48-9, *48-9*
    colour notes, 29
    gouache, 40
    palette, 49
    watercolour washes, 39
    watercolours, 34-6
composition, 52-5, *52-7*
Constable, John, *10*, 13, 44, 61-2, 94, 96
contre jour, 102
Corot, Jean-Baptiste Camille, 13
Cozens, John Robert, 10
Cuyp, Aelbert, 10

D
Degas, Edgar, 20, 22
donkeys, artists', 47, *47*
drawing boards, 47
drawings:
    enlarging, 29
    mounting and framing, 106
    for reference, 28-9, *28-9*
    sketchbooks, 30, *30-1*
    techniques, 18
    for watercolours, 36-7
Dürer, Albrecht, 9

E
easels, 46-7, *46-7*
Egypt (Ian Potts), 82, *82-3*
enlarging drawings, 29
equipment, *see* materials

F
felt-tipped pens, 25
filbert brushes, 32
Fisher, Rev. John, 94
fixatives:
    charcoal, 20
    pastels, 23
fountain pens, 25, *25*
framing, 106, *106-7*

G
Gauguin, Paul, 43
geology, 60-1
Gilpin, William, 55
Giorgione, 9
Girtin, Thomas, *9*, 10
glazes, acrylics, 45
Going Home, 57
Golden Section, *29*, 53
gouache, 23, *34*, 40, *40-1*
    mounting and framing, 106
graphite pencils, *18*, 19, *19*
graphite sticks, 19

H
hardboard supports, 43
Hardy, Thomas, 62
Hiler, Hilaire, 43
history, 8-13
Hobbema, Meindert, 10
hog's hair brushes, *32*
horizon, 53, *94*, 96
Hours of Turin, 8
Howard, Ken, *Beach Scenes*, 102, *102-5*

I
impasto, *44*, 45, *95*
Impressionists, 13

Indian ink, 25, *26*
ink drawings, 24-5, *24-7*

L
Landscape and Industry (Andrew Laws), 86, *86-9*
Laws, Andrew, *Landscape and Industry*, 86, *86-9*
laying a wash, 39
light:
    beach scenes, 102, *102-5*
    contre jour, 102
    mood and atmosphere and, 58, 61-2
Limbourg brothers, 8
linocuts, *56*
linseed oil, 43, 44
location painting, 64-5, *64-5*
Luttrell Psalter, 9

M
Martini, Simone, 8
masonite supports, 43
materials, 14
    acrylics, *44*, 45
    brushes, 32-3, *32-3*
    charcoal, 20, *20-1*
    easels, 46-7, *46-7*
    gouache, 40, *40-1*
    oils, 44-5, *45*
    paper, 16, *17*
    pastels, 22-3, *22-3*
    pen and ink, 24-5, *24-7*
    pencils, 18-19, *18-19*
    sketchbooks, 30, *30-1*
    supports, 42-3, *42-3*
    watercolour, 34-9, *34-9*
matting, 106, *106-7*
Monet, Claude, 13, 100
mood, 58, 62
mounting, 106, *106-7*
Murphy, Wendy, *Clouds, sky and the sea*, 94, *94-7*

N
Newton, Sir Isaac, 48
nibs, 25

O
oil pastels, 22, 23, *23*
oils, 44-5, *45*
    brushes, 32, 33
    framing, 106
    impasto, *95*
    supports, 43
open air painting, 64-5, *64-5*
ox-hair brushes, 32, *32*

P

paints:
　acrylics, *44*, 45
　oils, 44-5, *45*
　watercolour, 34-9, *34-9*
palette, colour, 49
paper:
　for pastels, 22-3
　sketchbooks, 30
　stretching, 16, *17*
　types, 16
Pasmore, Victor, 13, *13*
pastels, 22-3, *22-3*
　mounting and framing, 106
pen and ink, 24-5, *24-7*
pencils, 18-19, *18-19*
Pissarro, Camille, 13
plywood supports, 43
pointillism, *53*
poppy oil, 44
portable sketching easels, 47, *47*
Post-Impressionists, 13
Potts, Ian, *65*
　Athens, 80, *80-1*
　Egypt, 82, *82-3*
Poussin, Nicolas, 9-10, 13
priming canvases, 43
propelling pencils, 19

Q

quill pens, 25

R

radial easels, *46*, 47
reed pens, 25, *25*
Rembrandt, *8*, 10, 24
Renoir, Pierre Auguste, 13
rivers, 100, *100-1*
round brushes, 32
Ruskin, John, 90
Ruysdael, Salomon van, 10

S

sable brushes, 32, *32*, 33
scale, 52
seascapes:
　composition, 53
　skies, 94-6, *94-7*
　White Cliffs, 66, *66-71*
Seghers, Hercules, 10
Seurat, Georges, *53*
shapes, 58-60
size, primers, 43
sketchbooks, 30, *30-1*
sketching easels, 47, *47*
skies, 94-6, *94-7*
snow scenes, *63*, *99*
squirrel brushes, 32

starch, watercolour used with, *39*
stools, *47*
stretching canvases, 43
stretching paper, 16, *17*
structure, 58-60
students' colours, watercolours, 34
studio easels, *46*, 47
sunrises and sunsets, 62
supports, 42-3, *42-3*
Swiss Lakes, 72-3, *72-7*

T

table-top easels, 47
technical pens, 25
techniques:
　acrylics, *44*, 45
　charcoal, 20, *20-1*
　drawing, 18-19, *18-19*
　gouache, 40, *40-1*
　oils, 44-5, *45*
　pastels, 22-3, *22-3*
　pen and ink, 24-5, *24-7*
　watercolour, 34-9, *34-9*
tempera, 23
Thomas, Dylan, 62
tone:
　composition, 55
　watercolour washes, 39
torchons, *23*
Toulouse-Lautrec, Henri de, 43
Trant, Carolyn, *62*, *99*
trees, 98, *98-9*
Turner, Joseph Mallord William, *11*, 13, 24, 28, *34*, 39, 52, *60*, 61-2, 64, 73, 78, 96
turpentine, 43, 44
Tuscany, 84, *84-5*

U

underpaintings, 45

V

Valéry, Paul, 7
Van Eyck, Jan, 8
Van Gogh, Vincent, 13, 24, 44, 55
Venice, 78-9, *78-9*
Vicary, Richard, *56*
Vlieger, Simon, 10
Vollard, Ambroise, 22
Vuillard, Edouard, *12*, 40

W

washes, watercolour, 36, *36*, *38-9*, 39
water:
　lakes, 72-3, *72-7*

　rivers, 100, *100-1*
　see also seascapes
water-soluble pencils, 19
watercolours, 34-9, *34-9*
　brushes, 32
　inks, 25
　mounting and framing, 106
　used with gouache, 40
　washes, 36, *36*, *38-9*
wax resist, watercolour washes, *39*
weather, 58
wet-on-wet, *84*, *92*
White Cliffs, 66, *66-71*
window mounts, 106
Winter, William, 7
Wordsworth, William, 10

PICTURE CREDITS